"*The First Mess Cookbook* is not just an inspiring view into Laura Wright's productive kitchen and garden or simply a collection of truly delicious recipes; it is a comprehensive guide to creating healthy and irresistible plant-based meals every day."

—AMY CHAPLIN, James Beard Award–winning author of
At Home in the Whole Food Kitchen

"Laura Wright is a rare jewel, and her debut cookbook is no different. Shining with her creative spirit, each recipe is a celebration of beauty and abundance, living well, and eating well. Just by flipping through these pages, you are immediately aware of her reverence for fresh, healthy food and that each recipe is an ode to Earth's gifts."

—SARAH BRITTON, author of *My New Roots*

"Laura has a way of making plant-based food appeal to everyone, no matter their diet preferences. I will continue to reach for this book for everything from her amazing dairy-free coffee creamer to weeknight dinner ideas or something special for guests."

—SARA FORTE, author of *The Sprouted Kitchen*
and *Sprouted Kitchen: Bowl + Spoon*

"Laura is a plant-based culinary genius. Anyone desiring to add exciting new vegan recipes to their repertoire must have this book."

—DANA SHULTZ, *author of Minimalist Baker's Everyday Cooking*

"Laura Wright's *The First Mess Cookbook* is a soulful, sumptuous feast for the eyes and belly. Lush photographs and candid storytelling brings a rich collection of creative, plant-based recipes to life."

—GENA HAMSHAW, author of *Food52 Vegan*

"Laura's no-fuss, simple but stylish approach to healthy food is as bold as it is beautiful. Her magical mess is a joyful celebration of eating well and living well."

—TESS MASTERS, author of *The Blender Girl,*
The Blender Girl Smoothies, and *The Perfect Blend*

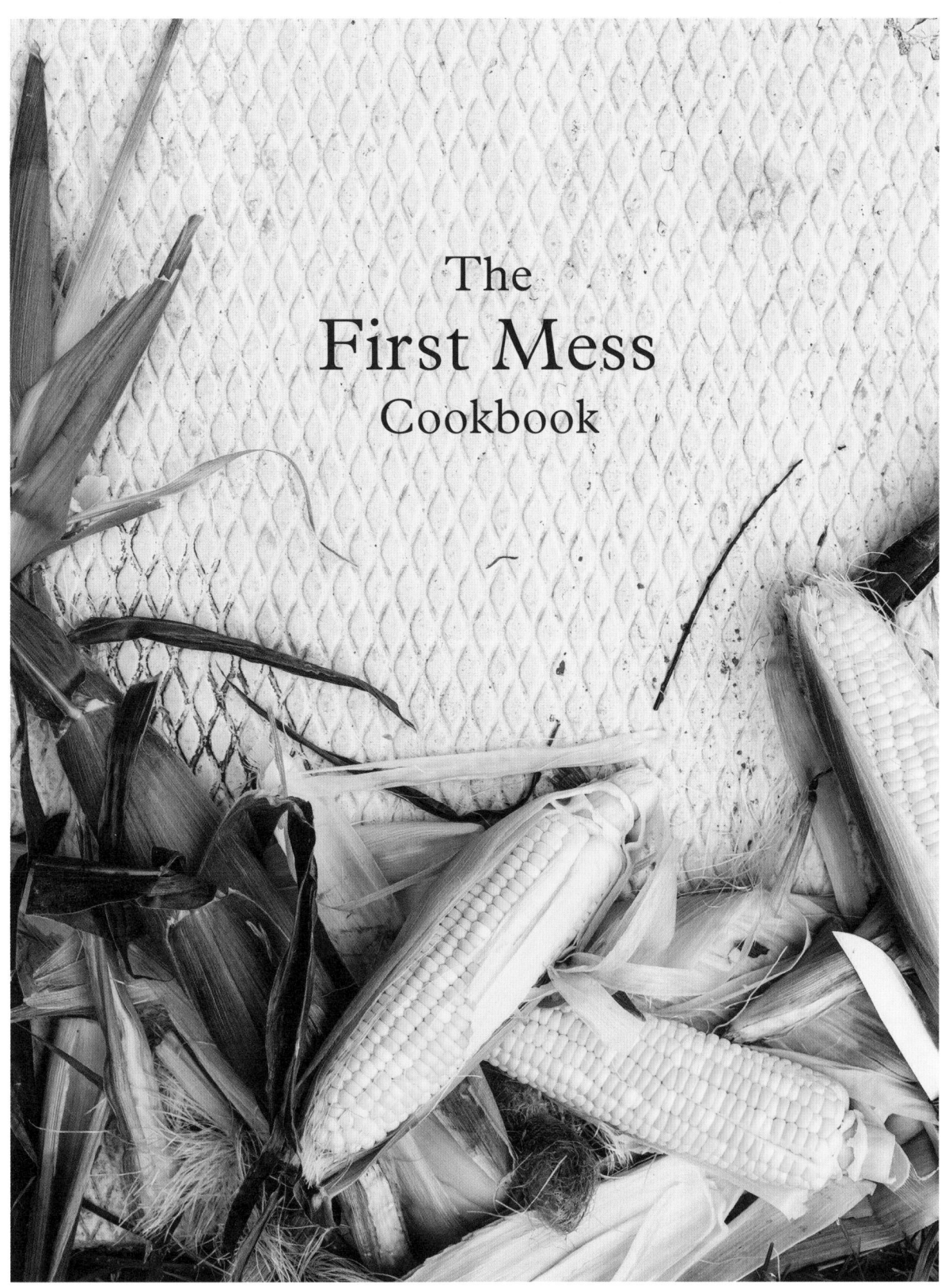

The
First Mess
Cookbook

The
FIRST
MESS
Cookbook

Vibrant Plant-Based Recipes
to Eat Well Through the Seasons

LAURA WRIGHT

AVERY
an imprint of Penguin Random House
New York

an imprint of Penguin Random House LLC
375 Hudson Street
New York, New York 10014

Most Avery books are available at special quantity discounts
for bulk purchase for sales promotions, premiums, fund-
raising, and educational needs. Special books or book
excerpts also can be created to fit specific needs. For details,
write SpecialMarkets@penguinrandomhouse.com.

ISBN 9781583335901

Printed in China
10 9 8 7 6 5 4 3 2 1

Book design by Jennifer Griffiths
Cover design by Jennifer Griffiths
Cover images by Laura Wright

For Mark, who takes all of my messy moments in stride.
Thank you for always making me laugh.

Contents

Vegetables and a Couple of Grains

Energizing Drinks and Small Bites

Desserts and Small Treats

Introduction

Raspberry picking throughout the humid Ontario summers was my first job as a youth, and I suppose this is where the inspiration for my blog, *The First Mess*, began. I would put on my rubber boots, grab a basket, and head toward the back of my parents, two-acre property in the country. At the end of the line were rows of raspberry bushes, heaving with fruit under the steamy July sun. One berry in the basket, one in my mouth. My brother and I would get two dollars for every pint we could scrounge up, and my dad would sell them at his farm market store the next day. I don't think I ever made more than ten dollars a pick. I was too busy eating those warm berries that tasted of jam, nectar, and light. That all-sensory field experience is my first clear memory of connecting to food beyond the notion of hunger being satisfied.

Throughout my adult life, food has continued to be a driving force of pride, success, and pleasure. I grew up with that farm market of my father's as a second home. Where some kids would go visit their grandmother for a nice dinner, I worked under the guidance of mine every week, learning about hard work and the drive to succeed for the sake of your family and your own personal wellness. She was a presence at the store into her 90th year because the dignity of work kept her going.

That farm market provided my first "real" job as a teenager, cashing out the locals who returned every week for fresh fruit and vegetables. My dad always told me to thank them sincerely as they left, because they were supporting our family, yes, but also because they were committing their dollars to the community and local food movement as well. My family hinged on that movement before it was a buzzword or topic in magazines. It was our life and sustenance in every way you could imagine.

At home, there were giant tomato plants, greens, runner beans, squash, and any fruit or vegetable that could take root in my father's hobby garden. We always had fresh, healthy food outside our door in the warm months and beautiful preserves in the colder times to remind us of preparation, knowledge, and hard work and its virtues. My mother and Nana made wholesome dinners from scratch every night of the week. When I pick up a knife in my own kitchen, I'm grateful for their persistence in keeping us well fed all those years, along with all the other amazing things they managed to do.

When I attended university to study environmental ethics, I examined virtue and intention in depth. Along with those themes came discussions of suffering, gluttony, factory farming and mono-crops, famine, societies that live and breathe with the land, freedom, commodity, and community feeling. Those liberal arts seminars always had me circling back to food, its deeply woven connection to life, and its global impact. With everything I had learned, I decided to go vegan. I was serving at a restaurant to pay my university tuition and trying out vegan recipes in my spare time when I realized my real calling in life.

I enrolled in a nutritional culinary management program a year later. In those classrooms, I learned how to sharpen my knife, convert ounces to grams, poach eggs, make pastry, clean and filet a whole fish, execute every vegetable cut, and how to understand the book of yields so that I wouldn't waste the money of my future employer. I lived for the nutritional cooking labs of that program because the modules lined up with my own plant-preferring ways. We would make fragrant Thai green curries with sprouted tofu, crusty loaves of bread with whole-grain flour, and creamy chocolate mousse out of avocados. I was in awe and inspired on a regular basis.

I worked for one of Canada's original farm-to-table chefs while I studied culinary arts. Just as with every restaurant I had worked in up to that point and continue to work in now, that's where my education was happening in real time. In those time-pressured and passionate environments, I learned that when serving others for a living, one is never too skilled or too advanced to slice a bushel of pears, scrub a stack of pots, or exercise empathy with an unhappy guest. If you want to inspire and nourish the community, those repetitive, and sometimes frustrating, tasks

are necessary. The day-to-day hard work gives meaning and substance to all the big things one can accomplish with food.

I learned a lot more about how people and families were eating at home when I volunteered at a community youth program that focused on empowering through cooking and food education. I realized that my own upbringing was, for the most part, quite unusual. The constant presence of fresh food, the every-night family dinners, a big garden in the summer, a loaded cellar in the winter, a job, a sense of community at the table—all were things that I may have been taking for granted. Through knife skills workshops, hummus-making demonstrations, and the chance to show teenagers the surprising goodness of tofu cooked intentionally, I could see and feel the positive shift toward the real, healthy, and homemade meals of my upbringing. I was excited and inspired by their enthusiasm once they were shown a different way. I fed off that energy and their recognition of something inherently good. I remained hopeful that their new appreciation for whole foods was a reflection of some greater changes in the world.

Not long after I finished culinary school and the volunteer gig, I started my blog, *The First Mess*, at the urging of friends. There were texts, phone calls, and face-to-face conversations about eating well. They would ask me how to make beets taste really good with minimal fuss, how I had been making almond milk at home, what was in that kale salad from the dinner party the other night, and how to even approach ingredients like tempeh and eggplant. One friend in particular kept urging me toward the start of a blog focused on the kind of food I had been making and eating; delicious, no-fuss, healthy, seasonal, and of course vegan.

Eating and living a plant-based existence had given me a lot: better energy, a renewed passion for cooking, a sense of clarity, and a higher purpose in everything else I did. I knew that sharing what I had learned in restaurants, at school, and from feeding people in general, could make for approachable, useful, and inspiring content online. I named my blog after a passage in M.F.K. Fisher's *An Alphabet for Gourmets*, where she discusses the first planting and "mess" of peas in the spring. She seemed to speak to all of the things I wanted to share—a reverence for something delicious that came from the earth, style in simplicity, seasonal eating, and that explicit connection between eating well and living well. The first comment I received on a post solidified my excitement that others were looking for the same level of inspiration that I was.

Many posts and a few years later, the words of encouragement I get from followers all over the world inspire me to create delicious plant-based recipes that anyone can make and feel good about. Going through my email inbox and the blog's comments section gives me that same inspired energy I felt in the kitchen of that volunteer program. The ongoing dialogue around living well for personal vibrancy, with carnivores and raw foodists alike, drives me to create better recipes that anyone can turn to for their own health, for the nourishment of their family, and to help celebrate their community.

On Eating Well with This Book

I find simple food to be the most satisfying, and it has a lot of style if you're mindful about the approach and presentation. This book has over one hundred vegan recipes that embody both earthy and elegant characteristics. These are the kinds of dishes that I prepare for myself and for guests. The food is comfortable and familiar but also special with a seasonal spin, an extra nourishing component, or a unique plant-based take.

My eating philosophy is definitively vegan and rooted in the seasons, but I also cook and eat for joy and happiness. A plant-based lifestyle in accordance with the Earth's rhythms makes me feel amazing, but with my blog and cooking in general, I always aim to inspire rather than preach about the virtues. Like omnivores and vegans alike, I eat for pleasure first and tend to gravitate toward a certain overall abundance with my food—in color, textural variation, and good flavor. When I keep these things in mind with my own cooking and recipes, I know that I'm creating something that transcends dietary and seasonal confines, even if it does play within them.

This book is divided into sections for easy navigating. Mornings and Breakfasts showcases some of my quiet weekday preparations, like simple bowls of grains or a cozy tea latte. I also give you a few brunch-appropriate dishes that call for a touch more effort and celebration. The Soups and Stews section features some of my favorite recipes in the book: filling one-pot meals and plenty of weeknight-easy recipes. The Salads and Dressings chapter focuses on salads that can be pumped up with a bit of protein and brought up to meal status. There are a few multi-purpose dressings in the mix with that chapter as well. Hearty Mains and Big Plates is the stuff that vegan dreams are made of. All the dishes in this section are great on their own with little to no need for sides. In the event that you want to fill out your plate with something extra, there's the Vegetables and a Couple of Grains section to cover all the bases. There are simple, but unique, vegetable preparations here that cover steaming, roasting, mashing, and fermenting. The Energizing Drinks and Small Bites section bridges the gap between meals with easy snacks, interesting appetizers, and some wellness drinks to keep you feeling bright. The sweet ending is Desserts and Small Treats. I have a range of sweets here, like scones or cookies to go with tea or more involved celebration desserts. There are gluten-free, grain-free, and cane sugar–free options for all palates with a few dessert basics to experiment with as well—things like lemon curd, whipped coconut cream, and basic vegan ice cream.

At the beginning of each recipe, these symbols will offer clarity on dietary designations and restrictions:

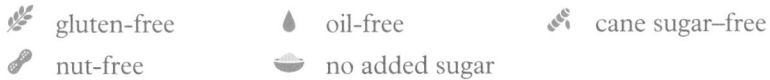

🌾 gluten-free   💧 oil-free   🌱 cane sugar–free

🥜 nut-free   🥣 no added sugar

I've also included a note when a recipe requires additional time for prep or to soak ingredients.

With big hugs and boundless gratitude,

xo Laura

Stocking Your Pantry for Success

Besides fresh, seasonal fruits and vegetables, the foundation of any vegan or vegetarian's lifestyle, you'll want to keep a few pantry items on hand when cooking recipes from this book. I've broken this section down into seven subsections: Healthy Fats and Oils, Acidity, Natural Sweeteners, Protein, Whole Grains, Baking Necessaries, and Flavor Savers.

Healthy Fats and Oils

People say all the time that fat is flavor, but that isn't technically true. Fat performs the crucial function of coating your palate and therefore merely *distributes* the flavor of what you're eating for optimal enjoyment. Some plant-based fats I use for their subtle flavor, but for the most part, they're a vehicle for the cooking process or a crucial component for creating a certain texture.

COCONUT OIL (REFINED AND VIRGIN)

I reach for refined coconut oil when I need the buttery texture of this rich oil to enhance a dessert. I use virgin coconut oil in dishes or desserts that will benefit from the outright coconut flavor (like the Coconut Cream Tart on page 247). I specify which one I use in each recipe.

OLIVE OIL

This is my main cooking oil of choice. I buy an organic, large bottle of it from Costco and refill a little cruet beside my stove for everyday use. Sometimes I splurge on regional or artisanal extra virgin varieties if I plan to enjoy them simply, such as drizzled over sliced summer tomatoes or as a complement to fresh sourdough bread.

GRAPESEED OR SUNFLOWER OIL

I keep both of these around because they remain liquid at room temperature, they can handle higher-heat cooking, and they have very little flavor. They are both also great for large batches of vinaigrettes because they won't solidify or turn your vinaigrette into Jell-O in the refrigerator.

RAW CASHEW AND OTHER NUT AND SEED BUTTERS

I use raw cashew butter for creamy dressings, to add an extra-rich, dairy-like touch to healthy desserts, or to just add a much-needed creaminess. Having a jar on hand is preferable and frankly more reliable (in my case) than remembering to soak cashews overnight. Other nut or seed butters I keep on hand include roasted and raw almond, hazelnut, sesame (tahini), and sunflower seed.

CANNED FULL-FAT COCONUT MILK

This ingredient makes so many plant-based desserts possible. Its richness mimics fatty dairy products, and you can even extract the top layer of cream from the can to whip for a delicious frosting or topping. With the whipping technique in mind, you'll want to take note of a few things while shopping for coconut milk. Grocery stores tend to run at cooler temperatures, so when you select a can, lightly shake it to detect the amount of cream solids within. If you hear plenty of sloshing and feel the movement, move on to the next one. The can should feel like one unified mass when shaken. Conversely, if you hear sloshing/detect movement, this type of can would be perfect for a recipe that requires the milk in its liquid state. Aside from desserts, I use coconut milk in smoothies, soups, and curries, and even as the base for dressings and sauces.

Acidity

Vinegars and citrus juice are necessary for balancing flavors in recipes. They contribute an essential brightness and often "wake up" dormant flavors in a dish.

LEMON AND LIME JUICE

Nature's most readily available acids, lemon and lime juices, are best straight from the fruit and squeezed right before you need them. I've found that squeezing a lemon even 30 minutes before I plan to use the juice weakens the potency of flavor. Although citrus is not local to me, it does seem to have a proper season around December to February.

RAW APPLE CIDER VINEGAR

This is the most diverse vinegar you can buy, and it's also quite healthy. I even drink it on a weekly basis as a revitalizing tonic of sorts (see the Turmeric Cider "Switchy" on page 209). Good apple cider vinegar will have cultural strands of the "mother" at the bottom of the bottle and will smell lightly sweet. When my local health food store sells out of an Ontario-based brand, I usually buy Bragg.

WHITE WINE VINEGAR AND BALSAMIC VINEGAR

Both of these vinegars function in specific contexts within this book. The white wine vinegar is used when I know the flavor of lemon will disappear and I need something lighter or more neutral than apple cider vinegar. I tend to use balsamic vinegar when I want a slightly sweet and deeper flavor note.

Natural Sweeteners

Sweetness is par for the course with desserts, but it's also surprisingly necessary for balance in savory plant-based dishes. A lot of my vinaigrettes feature a small amount of maple syrup, not because I want them to taste sweet, but because I need to emphasize the other flavors in the vinaigrette or salad. I avoid cane sugar because alternative sweeteners have a more interesting flavor, they contain additional nutrients, and they tend to be less processed. Here's a selection of the sweet things I employ in this book.

MEDJOOL DATES

These fudgy natural sugar bombs are like candy. I use them in no-bake desserts, as a binder in a raw cake batter, in healthy shakes and smoothies, as a sweetener for Vanilla Coconut Coffee Creamer (page 31), and even as a point of interest in savory stews with plenty of warm spices. If I'm hitting an afternoon slump and need a snack, I stuff one of these with a couple of salted almonds and call it a day.

PURE MAPLE SYRUP

This is probably my most reached-for sweetener and considering my country of origin, that can't be a surprise. Canada's flag is emblazoned with the maple leaf, so my loyalty to the syrup runs deep. I always choose a deep amber, Grade B variety, and I use it in many things. This boiled sap of maple trees contains trace minerals too, so pour a little extra on your oatmeal next time.

MAPLE AND COCONUT PALM SUGAR

Sometimes a granulated sweetener is necessary for structure in a dessert, and for those times, I reach for maple sugar or coconut palm sugar. I realize that maple sugar may not be available everywhere, and even when it is available, it can be quite expensive. Any time I specify maple sugar, coconut palm sugar will sub in, one for one, in its place.

I use these sweeteners decidedly less often. Brown rice syrup has a strong flavor and mostly serves as a sticky salve for things like granola bars in my kitchen. Agave nectar can be quite refined and therefore, it absorbs like a mega dose of unadulterated natural sugar. I only use it when I need the most subtle-tasting sweetener possible. It's also a preferable choice for sweetening beverages because it mingles with the liquid effortlessly, like simple syrup.

Protein

Beans, legumes, tempeh, tofu, nuts, seeds, whole grains, and even vegetables all contain plant-based protein. Some sources and combinations are more complete than others, but rest assured that your body knows how to take all your varied protein components and turn them into a whole. Here's a rundown of the sources I cook with most often.

BEANS

There are hundreds of bean varieties. My core rotation has black beans, some type of kidney bean, cannellini or navy beans, and mung beans for sprouting. I try to cook my beans from dry as often as possible because I find they really do taste better. I always keep canned varieties on hand for last-minute cooking endeavors.

LEGUMES

Chickpeas are my favorite concentrated plant source. I cook and eat them at least once a week. I also keep split red lentils on hand for dips and dal, and French or black beluga lentils for applications that require a bit more bite, like salads.

TEMPEH AND TOFU

These are both soy based (one is a fermented soy cake and the other is soy curd, essentially) and very high in protein. I always aim to buy organic, non-GMO soy products. Tempeh benefits from a 10-minute steam before you cook or marinate it to open up its "pores" to any seasoning. I always buy sprouted tofu in "extra firm" because I find the texture of this product to be the most appealing and appropriate for my preferred cooking methods.

I treat these more like protein accents since the fat content of nuts and seeds makes dishes quite rich when they are used in large quantity. Some nuts and seeds that I always have on hand: almonds, cashews, hazelnuts, pecans, pine nuts, peanuts, sunflower seeds, pumpkin seeds, sesame seeds, flaxseeds, hulled hemp hearts, and chia seeds. I keep a small amount of each one at room temperature, and store the rest in sealed bags in the freezer for longer shelf life.

Whole Grains

I need some kind of whole grain with almost every meal to feel satisfied. Whether it's a steamy heap of brown basmati rice or a slice of sprouted grain bread for my Old Reliable Avocado Toast (page 62), I make room for grains on my plate, always. Surprisingly, grains can go stale or off-tasting, so I always find it economically advantageous to buy smaller amounts in bulk to minimize waste.

The gluten-free grains that I keep on hand include raw buckwheat groats, certified gluten-free rolled oats and steel-cut oats, quinoa, millet, popping corn, brown basmati rice, and wild rice blends.

Some gluten-containing grains I keep on hand are sprouted wheat bread (such as Ezekiel), spelt pasta in a variety of shapes, and whole farro.

Baking Necessaries

I try to avoid refined flour and sugar in my baking because I think treats can have an element of virtue to them if you try hard enough. For this reason, I don't stock white flour or refined cane sugar in my pantry. Because my lifestyle is vegan, I don't turn to butter or eggs either. This often means that I have to get creative with plant-based ingredients. Here are a few things I've learned to keep around through trial and error.

GLUTEN-CONTAINING FLOUR

Sprouted whole spelt flour is my kitchen's version of all-purpose flour. I love its nutty taste and find it to be quite diverse for whole-grain flour. I've had better luck with the sprouted version of whole spelt flour. It tastes cleaner and makes for lighter baked goods.

GLUTEN-FREE FLOURS

I'm not a gluten-free baking expert, and I don't have a gluten sensitivity myself. I do keep a decent rotation of gluten-free flours on hand for when I need to do some internet recipe research and make something gluten-free for others. I always buy these flours in small quantities at the bulk store because I never know when I'll use one or the other next. Some of the more common gluten-free flours I use are almond flour, coconut flour, brown rice flour, chickpea flour, buckwheat flour, certified gluten-free oat flour, and millet flour. I make my own buckwheat, oat, and millet flour by grinding whole grains in my blender as I need them.

VEGAN EGGS

Of course, there's no such thing as a vegan egg, but there are a variety of good, whole-food egg replacements. I use unsweetened applesauce and mashed banana in cookies and cakes. One tablespoon of ground chia seeds or flaxseeds combined with filtered water works well to bind pancakes, waffles, and cookies. Arrowroot powder or flour is something I turn to often to perform the function of eggs. It acts like cornstarch essentially, binding and thickening whatever it's added to. You have to be careful to not overheat arrowroot though, as it can break down and have the reverse effect of thinning a batter or sauce.

ALUMINUM-FREE BAKING POWDER

Since I don't use eggs and therefore rely on baking powder for extra lift in my baked goods, I always choose an aluminum-free one. Consuming aluminum has been linked to quite a few health maladies, but conventional baking powder also lends a bitter taste to baked goods if used in higher quantity. I buy my aluminum-free baking powder from Bob's Red Mill.

CHOCOLATE

I buy the most ethically produced vegan chocolate and cocoa powder that I can afford and always triple check the label for dairy and excessive added sugar when I'm buying semi-sweet chips or chunks. Buying a dark chocolate bar and chopping it up is usually the best bet for transparency in terms of how the chocolate was produced and what it contains. Cocoa powder should always be unsweetened.

VANILLA

Vanilla is an ingredient that I take seriously. I buy it in beans, powdered form, and extract. I find that vegan baking with wholesome ingredients requires extra vanilla to round out and soften the flavors of whole-grain flours and less refined sweeteners. My friend Ashlae makes high-quality vanilla extract that's so popular, she usually sells out within a day of its release. When I can't get hers, I buy Nielsen-Massey brand.

Flavor Savers

This is the most important ingredient category of all. Along with herbs and spices, there are certain ingredients that I use because they have the all-important umami flavor—the definitively savory fifth taste. Here's an outline of what I keep in my refrigerator and pantry.

MISO

Miso is a fermented soybean paste that is most often used in a simple broth-based soup. You can buy versions made from chickpeas, barley, and rice as well. It has a very complex flavor that varies by type, but I would say the dominant characteristics are salty, meaty, and nutty. I generally stock the mellow or white variety because I find it to be the most diverse.

GLUTEN-FREE TAMARI SOY SAUCE

Tamari is a rich, naturally fermented soy sauce. Again, it has a top note of saltiness that adds depth and balance to foods almost instantly. Be mindful of how much salt and pepper you use in recipes with tamari listed as an ingredient.

MUSTARD

It's not just a topping for veggie burgers—I put mustard in and on all kinds of things. It's my emulsifier of choice for vinaigrettes, I season soups with it, and I incorporate it into batters and dough. I keep Dijon, whole grain, and yellow mustard on hand at all times. I also use whole mustard seeds (yellow and black) in curries and spice mixtures.

TOMATO PASTE

I use this to heighten the richness of tomato dishes, of course. Strangely enough though, this economical paste also works in recipes where I'm not aiming for a tomato essence per se but feel that I need something extra or deeper in flavor. Raw tomatoes are naturally rich in umami flavor, so when you take that characteristic and concentrate it times one hundred, you have a very special ingredient. I buy the kind that comes in a tube for easy dispensing when I need it.

NUTRITIONAL YEAST

This flaked condiment is a miracle for the dairy-averse. It tastes mildly cheesy and so savory. If you buy a good brand, it will also be fortified with vitamin B12, which is important for vegans and vegetarians. Just remember to always keep your nutritional yeast in a cool, dark place because vitamin B12 is sensitive to light. Red Star and Bragg both make a good one.

HERBS AND SPICES

In the warm months, I grow every variety of fresh herb I can get my hands on because I have the space and honestly, they don't need a lot of care to thrive—just a good amount of sunlight and frequent trimming. When winter sets in, I buy a tight selection at the store. Here are the ones I like to keep around almost all of the time: thyme, flat-leaf parsley, chives, and cilantro. The following herbs I purchase less frequently and usually have a specific purpose in mind when I buy them: dill, mint, rosemary, and basil.

I don't mind using dried herbs at all. I keep dried thyme, oregano, and bay leaves on hand, and I use them often.

For spices, I tend to buy whole and ground ones in small amounts because they go bad and taste like nothing after about 6 months. Some of my most used ones are sweet paprika, smoked paprika, ground and whole cumin, ground and whole coriander, ground turmeric, ground sumac, garlic powder, and baking spices like whole nutmeg, cinnamon, and powdered ginger.

I have a select group of blended spices that I use often as well: mild curry powder, Old Bay seasoning, and za'atar.

Kitchen Equipment for Eating Well

Once you start making more of your own food from scratch with seasonal produce, you may need to start slowly investing in more kitchen equipment to increase your repertoire and to open the door to more variety in the recipes you can take on. That's not to say that you have to spend a fortune. Some of these tools I suggest below are quite inexpensive and very diverse in their capability. You may even have these items in your kitchen already. I've broken down my equipment of choice into three categories for this book: Necessary, Nice to Have, and Deluxe Commitment.

Necessary

KNIVES

Sturdy and sharp knives that feel good in your hand turn cooking as a task into cooking for pleasure. Plant-based cooking from natural, seasonal ingredients requires plenty of knife work, so take the time to find knives you like. I have an 8-inch (20 cm) chef's knife, a paring knife, and a long, serrated knife for bread.

POTS AND PANS

My fundamental pot selection is as follows: a 2-quart (2 L) saucepan, 10-inch and 12-inch (25 and 30 cm) ovenproof sauté pans, and a 7-quart (7 L) Dutch oven or other heavy-bottomed pot with a tight-fitting lid. This is all you really need.

HALF-SHEET PANS

These pans always accommodate exactly what I need and parchment paper rolls seem to be sized specifically for them, which is great for easy clean-up. I buy them at the restaurant supply store for the best value and durability.

MIXING AND PREP BOWLS

I prefer to lay out all my ingredients in prepped and chopped form before I actually start cooking, so I have a solid selection of tiny and large bowls for all my potential ingredients. Nesting bowls of medium and large size are great for salads, baking, and collecting vegetable scraps as you chop.

MICROPLANE GRATER OR RASP

I use a Microplane grater for a number of ingredients that I use often: citrus zest, fresh ginger, and garlic. It's especially helpful for the garlic because it eliminates the possibility of a guest chomping down on a large piece. A Microplane grater is also necessary for grating whole nutmeg, which is superior in flavor to pre-ground.

A BASIC DECENT BLENDER

Having a good blender has streamlined much of my prep work in the kitchen. I make all of my vinaigrettes and sauces in it. I can purée seasonal soups, and when I'm not in the mood to cook, a smoothie full of easily had, plant-based nutrients is always a possibility.

FINE-MESH STRAINER

This tool helps for draining cooked vegetables and pasta, but the fine mesh also makes it perfect for rinsing small grains like quinoa. I also strain my homemade plant-based milks with this style of strainer.

THE TRULY BASIC

Dry measuring cups, liquid measuring cups, measuring spoons, a steamer basket for vegetables, a box grater, a 2-slice toaster, nonreactive baking dishes, rubber spatulas, whisks, wooden spoons, and extra soup spoons for scooping up ingredients: these are all very useful, inexpensive things to keep on hand.

Nice to Have

FOOD PROCESSOR

This appliance is almost necessary to me. I use it to make piecrusts, tart fillings, truffles, sauces, pesto, purées, ice cream, and the list goes on. I've had the same budget model for years and it hasn't failed me, even with long streaks of daily use. You can even use it as a chopper and shredder if you don't feel like exercising your knife skills with certain recipes.

10-QUART (10 L) STOCKPOT

I think that good vegetable stock is fundamental to plant-based cooking, so one year I splurged on a huge stock pot that sits on my top open shelf in the kitchen. Sometimes when you have a piece of gear that is specifically made for one thing, if you keep it in view, you'll use it more often. That's exactly what happened when I bought this pot. I make one huge potful a month and I have stock for all the soups I could imagine.

MANDOLINE SLICER

I almost put this low-tech gadget in the Necessary category. It makes quick work of produce for slaws and especially pretty salads. I've had my inexpensive Benriner model for years and it's still incredibly sharp.

DIGITAL KITCHEN SCALE

I specify weight measures with some of the produce items in this book, and scales can be nice to have around in general for the sake of accuracy. You can always use the scale that they have at the grocery store before you buy your produce to make sure that you'll have the right amount.

SPICE GRINDER

This item will be sold as a coffee grinder as well. I use my spice grinder to unlock the flavor of whole spices whenever I can. Ground spices are very convenient when you're cooking spontaneously, but the flavor from freshly ground whole spices is always going to be superior. Once I clean it out after grinding spices, I use it for small batches of chia seeds and flaxseeds as well.

LARGE GLASS TUPPERWARE CONTAINERS

I keep these on hand so that I can hold over large batches of soup or cooked grains/beans, and then transfer them to the refrigerator for use throughout the week. If you can see what's in the container, it's a lot easier to come up with a plan for how you're going to use it and eat it up.

JULIENNE PEELER

I bought one of these on a whim for seven dollars and I haven't looked back. It sounds corny, but it's so much fun to make vegetables and fruit into noodles with this gadget. Sometimes I make a plate of noodles outright with it (like with the Sesame Cucumber Noodles with Melon and Avocado on page 121), and sometimes I like to just integrate strands of vegetable in with regular pasta for a vitamin boost. There are plenty of experimental rewards for such a small investment here.

Deluxe Commitment

HIGH-SPEED BLENDER

This is a holy grail item for plenty of health-conscious cooks who want to up their game, and for good reason. I've had my Vitamix blender for over 10 years now and I still use it at least once every day. It makes the best green smoothies (no bits to chew!), the creamiest soups, homemade nut butter and nut milk, flavorful sauces and vinaigrettes in a flash, and a host of other things. I would be lost without mine.

ATTRACTIVE CONTAINERS FOR WHOLE GRAINS AND OTHER DRY GOODS

Once I started placing my bulk bin items in dedicated containers that I kept in my line of sight, I started cooking with them more. I used to just keep a jumble of poorly labeled plastic bags in one drawer, and over time these mystery bags would go into the garbage. After stashing them, I'd forget that I had purchased them and that they even existed. After realizing I had three bags of buckwheat flour in that drawer, I went online and bought a variety of canisters so that I could get organized. I haven't thrown out pantry stock since.

A VEGETABLE GARDEN

I know some people are restricted by their living space or climate with this one, but if you have the opportunity, I urge you to try vegetable gardening as a hobby. Of course, it's an economical and empowering means of feeding yourself, but it also drives home the notions of patience, seasonality, and respect for the food supply chain. We eat well because of my vegetable garden, but it also makes me a better person.

Mornings & Breakfasts

Early morning is my favorite time of the day. I savor the quiet of the house and the neighborhood in general. I get into phases with my breakfast foods, choosing cool things with plenty of local fruit in the summers, and different styles of porridge or pancakes in the cold months. On the opposite end of early morning meals, there's brunch, which is my most preferred meal to entertain with. To start, it's lower pressure than a Friday night dinner. Everyone is bright and full of energy when they arrive because the weekend has them in a good mood. Guests are free to go about their day when the meal's over, too. There's plenty of variety in this section to suit your own quiet breakfasts or your rousing weekend get-togethers.

Early Morning Earl Grey

SERVES *1*   FREE OF 🌿🌾

This cozy drink pulls me out of bed most mornings. It's just the right amount of caffeine to get the day started. A few years ago, I got into an expensive Earl Grey latte habit and knew that I needed a more practical and less sugary solution. Blending the hot tea and almond milk with some coconut butter gives you that creamy, latte-like cap that's just so comforting and familiar. Coconut butter is a product that contains both the flesh and oil of the coconut.

1. Steep the Earl Grey tea in the boiling water for 4 minutes. Strain and set aside.

2. In a small saucepan over medium heat, bring the unsweetened almond milk to a gentle boil. Pour the hot milk into a blender. To the milk, add the strained Earl Grey tea, vanilla, maple syrup, and coconut butter.

3. Blend the mixture, slowly bringing it up to high speed, for about 30 seconds. Pour the hot mixture into a mug and enjoy immediately.

1 tablespoon (15 mL) loose-leaf Earl Grey tea (or 2 teabags)

¾ cup (175 mL) boiling water

¾ cup (175 mL) unsweetened almond milk

½ teaspoon (2 mL) pure vanilla extract

1 teaspoon (5 mL) pure maple syrup

1 teaspoon (5 mL) coconut butter

Mango Ginger Kombucha Mimosas

SERVES *8*   FREE OF 🌿 🥜 💧

I love serving these along with a very high-vibe brunch. It looks and drinks like a mimosa, but it has a little more going on flavor-wise from all the ginger and lime. Also, a health-supporting and lively tonic served in a champagne flute or cocktail glass seems to hit most people the right way on the weekend. If I plan to serve these, I make the mango purée the night before so that I can portion, pour, and go the next morning.

1. In a medium saucepan over medium heat, combine the mango, ginger, water, and maple syrup. Bring to a boil and then lower the heat to a simmer. Cook until the mango is noticeably mushier, about 3 minutes. Scrape the contents of the saucepan into a blender.

2. Add the lime juice to the blender, and whiz on high until you have a smooth purée. You can fine strain the purée if you like.

3. Portion 1 tablespoon (15 mL) of mango purée into each glass. Divide the ginger kombucha among the glasses. Serve each drink with a lime wedge.

1 cup (250 mL) chopped fresh mango (or thawed frozen mango chunks)

½-inch (1 cm) piece of fresh ginger, peeled and minced

2 tablespoons (30 mL) filtered water

½ teaspoon (2 mL) pure maple syrup

1 tablespoon (15 mL) fresh lime juice

3 cups (750 mL) ginger-flavored kombucha, chilled

8 lime wedges, for serving

Cookies for Breakfast

MAKES *12 cookies*   FREE OF

Most mornings I wake up early enough to sit down and enjoy my breakfast at home while I read the news. On those odd days when I find myself flying out the door, these cookies work nicely. They're *just* sweet enough to feel like a treat and quite good when dunked into hot coffee. The outer part of the cookie has a nice crispness while the inner cookie is similar to a hearty, whole-grain muffin—specifically the top part of the muffin, which everyone knows is the best part.

1. Preheat the oven to 350°F (180°C). Line a baking sheet with parchment paper and set aside.

2. In a large bowl, stir together the rolled oats, cinnamon, baking soda, sea salt, almond flour, and brown rice flour until combined.

3. In the bowl of a food processor, combine the mashed banana, almond butter, maple syrup, ground flaxseed, coconut oil, and vanilla. Process on high until the mixture is smooth.

4. Scrape the almond butter mixture into the large bowl with the oats and flour mixture. Throw your add-ins into the bowl. Stir the mixture with a spatula until you have a unified and very stiff cookie dough.

5. Drop 2 tablespoons (30 mL) of dough per cookie onto the prepared baking sheet. Flatten each mound of dough with the palm of your hand. Slide the baking sheet into the oven and bake until lightly golden brown, about 15 to 17 minutes. Cool cookies completely before storing in an airtight container. These will last on the counter for 5 days. You can also wrap each cookie individually with plastic wrap and freeze them. I place all the wrapped cookies in a resealable bag and defrost them as needed.

1¼ cups (300 mL) certified gluten-free rolled oats (not quick-cooking)

1 teaspoon (5 mL) ground cinnamon

½ teaspoon (2 mL) baking soda

½ teaspoon (2 mL) fine sea salt

½ cup (125 mL) almond flour

¼ cup (50 mL) brown rice flour

½ cup (125 mL) mashed ripe banana (about 1 large banana)

½ cup (125 mL) smooth almond butter, stirred

3 tablespoons (45 mL) pure maple syrup

2 tablespoons (30 mL) ground flaxseed

3 tablespoons (45 mL) liquid virgin coconut oil

1 teaspoon (5 mL) pure vanilla extract

1 cup (250 mL) add-ins of your choice (I like a mix of dried blueberries, pumpkin seeds, and chopped walnuts)

Vanilla Coconut Coffee Creamer

MAKES *2 cups (500 mL)*   FREE OF 🌿 🥜 🥥

When I first went vegan, I wasn't a coffee drinker. But when coffee did come into my life and I craved something creamy to mellow it out, I was at a bit of a loss. Plain almond milk wasn't getting the job done and purchasing supermarket dairy-free creamers was getting expensive (plus they tended to have more sugar than I liked). This seemed like something that could be easily fixed in a homemade way, so I started experimenting with canned full-fat coconut milk as the base. The inclusion of oil is necessary as it keeps the creamer from separating after it's introduced to hot liquid.

After many experiments, I've found that certain brands of coconut milk are better suited to this recipe as they are more likely to remain liquid after being chilled. Grocery stores tend to be on the cool side, so when you're there picking up coconut milk for this, shake the cans a bit to see if you can hear the milk sloshing around. If the contents seem quite liquid, it's probably a good bet for this recipe.

6 Medjool dates, pitted

1 can (13.5 ounces/400 mL) full-fat coconut milk

2 teaspoons (10 mL) pure vanilla extract

1 tablespoon (15 mL) sunflower oil (or other neutral-flavored oil that is liquid at room or cool temperatures)

tiny pinch of fine sea salt

1.   If your dates are very soft, proceed to the next step. If your dates are a little dry, place them in a small bowl and cover them in boiling water for 5 to 10 minutes. Thoroughly drain the dates.

2.   In a blender, combine the pitted dates, coconut milk, vanilla, sunflower oil, and sea salt. Blend on high until you have a smooth and thick liquid with minimal chunks of date visible.

3.   Over a medium bowl, strain the creamer with a fine-mesh strainer. Store the strained creamer in a jar with a tight-fitting lid. Keep the jar of creamer in the refreigerator. Shake to combine before using. The creamer will keep for roughly 1 week.

Fresh, Instant Almond Milk

MAKES *1 ⅔ cups (400 mL)*   FREE OF 🌿 🥜

Many big brand-name almond milks contain a whole lot of water, some thickeners, and sugar in place of the actual almonds. I have a high-speed blender, so the ability to make fresh milk from raw almonds is within reach, but I rarely have the headspace to think about soaking the almonds overnight. Now, I keep a jar of raw almond butter on hand and I never go without fresh almond milk. Once you've measured the ingredients, the work is done.

3 tablespoons (45 mL) raw almond butter

1½ cups (375 mL) filtered water

⅛ teaspoon (0.5 mL) sea salt

2 teaspoons (10 mL) pure maple syrup (optional)

¼ teaspoon (1 mL) pure vanilla extract (optional)

1. Combine the almond butter, water, sea salt, maple syrup, if using, and vanilla, if using, in a blender, and whiz on high until smooth and creamy. You can fine strain the milk if you like, but it isn't necessary. Almond milk will keep in the refrigerator for up to 1 week. Shake well before serving.

Mocha Hemp Fuel

MAKES *3 cups (750 mL)*   FREE OF 🌿 🥜 🌾

Caffeine, protein, and healthy fat form this perfect trifecta of breakfast fuel, along with a chocolaty bonus. In the summer months, when I have cold-brewed coffee concentrate on hand, I use about half the amount of coffee specified, and I add a bunch of ice to make this creamy and frothy. It veers over to the indulgent side, but some mornings that seems like just the ticket.

1. Combine the hemp seeds, water, coffee, maple syrup, vanilla, cocoa powder, and coconut oil, if using, in a high-speed blender and whiz on high until smooth and creamy. If you like, you can fine strain the mixture. This milk will keep in the refrigerator for up to 1 week. Shake well before serving.

½ cup (125 mL) hulled hemp seeds

2 cups (500 mL) filtered water

1 cup (250 mL) brewed and cooled coffee

2 tablespoons (30 mL) pure maple syrup

1 teaspoon (5 mL) pure vanilla extract

2 tablespoons (30 mL) unsweetened cocoa powder

1 teaspoon (5 mL) virgin coconut oil (optional)

Fluffiest Multigrain Pancakes

MAKES *9 pancakes*   FREE OF 🥜

For a time, I worked the front of house in a farm-to-table restaurant on most weekend nights. Weekend mornings were usually groggy, but I always made a big breakfast. My partner and I usually lean toward the sweet side of things on a slow morning, and I've been tweaking these pancakes over many lazy Sundays. I keep whole-grain flours in my kitchen almost exclusively, which can pose a challenge when trying to achieve lightness in texture. Using sprouted spelt flour and apple cider vinegar in addition to baking powder makes these pancakes puff up nicely.

1. Preheat the oven to 275°F (140°C). Place a baking sheet in the oven.

2. In a large bowl, combine the spelt flour, millet flour, oat flour, coconut palm sugar, baking powder, and sea salt.

3. In a medium bowl, vigorously whisk together the almond milk, apple cider vinegar, and ground chia seeds. The mixture should appear foamy on the top. Sometimes I run this through the blender to make sure the chia seeds are fully incorporated into the liquid.

4. Add the almond milk mixture to the dry ingredients in the large bowl. Then, add the orange juice, water, vanilla, and sunflower oil. Gently mix the batter together with a fork. It should be mostly combined with lumps and dry flour bits throughout. Avoid overmixing.

5. Let the batter sit for about 10 minutes while you heat a large skillet. A touch above medium heat is ideal for these pancakes.

6. When you're ready to make the pancakes, lightly grease the skillet, and drop the batter in by the ⅓ cup (75 mL). You should hear a moderate sizzle. Gently spread the pancake batter with a spatula. Cook the pancakes until dry around the edges, with bubbles popping through the surface, about 1 minute. The pancakes should be lightly browned on the underside. Flip the pancakes over and cook another 45 seconds to 1 minute.

7. Keep the pancakes warm on the baking sheet in the oven while you repeat this process with the remaining batter, using more oil to cook the pancakes if you find it necessary.

8. Serve pancakes with fruit, maple syrup, coconut butter, and other toppings of your choice.

½ cup (125 mL) whole spelt flour

½ cup (125 mL) millet flour

½ cup (125 mL) oat flour

1 tablespoon (15 mL) coconut palm sugar OR maple sugar

1½ tablespoons (22 mL) aluminum-free baking powder

½ teaspoon (2 mL) fine sea salt

1 cup (250 mL) unsweetened almond milk

2 teaspoons (10 mL) apple cider vinegar

1 tablespoon (15 mL) ground chia seeds

¼ cup (50 mL) fresh orange juice

¼ cup (50 mL) filtered water

1 teaspoon (5 mL) pure vanilla extract

2 tablespoons (30 mL) sunflower oil (or other neutral-flavored oil), plus extra for cooking

FOR SERVING

sliced fresh fruit or whole berries

pure maple syrup

coconut butter

other toppings of your choice

Maple-Spice Buckwheat Crispies Cereal

MAKES *about 5 cups (1.25 L)*   FREE OF 🌾 🥜   REQUIRES *time to soak*

Like a lot of kids, my school-morning breakfast was cereal and milk. I don't crave that combination often now, but when I do, I'm usually seeking some familiarity and routine. The warm spices and nutty, toasted flavor of this are deeply comforting with a generous pour of Fresh, Instant Almond Milk (page 32).

Soaking the buckwheat is important for the preparation because it softens the grain, but it also unleashes its gelling power. Combine that power with a sticky mix of maple syrup and granulated maple sugar, and you've got a cereal that would rival any grocery store option.

1. Preheat the oven to 325°F (160°C). Line a large baking sheet with parchment paper and set aside.

2. Lay out a clean kitchen towel or a couple of lengths of doubled paper towels. In a fine-mesh strainer, rinse the buckwheat groats thoroughly. You're aiming to remove as much of the slimy soaking liquid as possible. Scrape the rinsed buckwheat groats onto the clean kitchen towel and spread them out. Lightly pat the buckwheat groats dry and then transfer them to a large bowl.

3. To the large bowl, add the sliced almonds, coconut flakes, sunflower seeds, chia seeds, maple sugar, sea salt, cinnamon, ginger, and nutmeg. Toss everything to coat.

4. In a small bowl, whisk together the coconut oil, maple syrup, and vanilla, and then pour that over the buckwheat groats mixture. Stir with a rubber spatula to coat.

5. Scrape the wet cereal mixture onto the prepared baking sheet. Flatten and spread everything out with the back of your spatula as much as possible. Slide the baking sheet into the oven and bake for 50 minutes, stirring and flipping the crispies a few times to ensure even browning. Once the cereal is evenly golden brown and lightly crispy, it's ready.

6. Allow the cereal to cool completely before storing in a sealed container at room temperature. This cereal will keep for about 10 days.

---

1 cup (250 mL) raw buckwheat groats, soaked for at least 1 hour

1 cup (250 mL) sliced almonds

1 cup (250 mL) large-flake coconut

½ cup (125 mL) raw sunflower seeds

2 tablespoons (30 mL) chia seeds

3 tablespoons (45 mL) maple sugar OR coconut palm sugar

¼ teaspoon (1 mL) fine sea salt

1½ teaspoons (7 mL) ground cinnamon

¼ teaspoon (1 mL) ground ginger

¼ teaspoon (1 mL) ground nutmeg

2 tablespoons (30 mL) liquid virgin coconut oil

¼ cup (50 mL) pure maple syrup

1 teaspoon (5 mL) pure vanilla extract

Easy Gluten-Free Waffles

MAKES *6 large waffles*   FREE OF 🌿 🌾

These waffles have perfect crisp edges and tender centers, all with using fairly common gluten-free ingredients. The warm sweetness of the banana combined with the shredded coconut gives these waffles a bit of a macaroon vibe, which I really enjoy on those mornings when I'm craving something especially sweet. I find that they need barely a slick of maple syrup on top because they taste so good on their own.

It's important to grease your waffle iron before you pour the batter for each waffle with this recipe. The almond meal contributes a lovely moist texture, but it also makes these a touch more prone to sticking. If you generally prefer lighter waffles, note that these perform better on a darker, more cooked waffle iron setting.

1. Preheat the oven to 275°F (140°C). Place a baking sheet in the oven.

2. In a large bowl, whisk together the almond flour, oat flour, shredded coconut, baking powder, arrowroot powder, cinnamon, and sea salt.

3. In a blender or food processor, combine the ground flaxseed, mashed banana, almond milk, coconut oil, maple syrup, and vanilla. Mix on high for a minute or so. You want to activate the gelling power of the flaxseeds. The mixture should appear foamy.

4. Add the flax and banana mixture to the dry ingredients and gently stir until just combined. Let the batter sit for 12 to 15 minutes.

5. Heat your waffle iron to a setting in the higher range. I find a slightly hotter setting works best for these. Once the machine is ready, grease the irons with a bit of coconut oil using either a pastry brush or a wad of paper towel. Drop ½ cup (125 mL) of the batter into the center of the bottom iron and close the lid. Remove the waffle when the timer goes off or the waffle appears golden brown all across the top.

6. Keep the cooked waffles warm on the baking sheet in the oven while you repeat the cooking process with the remaining batter.

7. Serve waffles with nut or seed butter, fresh fruit, maple syrup, or any other accompaniments you enjoy.

1 cup (250 mL) almond flour

1¼ cups (300 mL) certified gluten-free oat flour

½ cup (125 mL) finely shredded unsweetened coconut

2 teaspoons (10 mL) aluminum-free baking powder

1½ teaspoons (7 mL) arrowroot powder

1 teaspoon (5 mL) ground cinnamon

½ teaspoon (2 mL) fine sea salt

2 tablespoons (30 mL) ground flaxseed

½ cup (125 mL) mashed ripe banana (approximately 1 large banana)

1¼ cups (300 mL) unsweetened almond milk

2 tablespoons (30 mL) liquid virgin coconut oil

1 tablespoon (15 mL) pure maple syrup

1 teaspoon (5 mL) pure vanilla extract

FOR SERVING

nut or seed butter

sliced fresh fruit or whole berries

pure maple syrup

others toppings of your choice

Savory Ginger Green Onion Crepes

MAKES *8 crepes*   FREE OF 🌿 🥜 🍚   REQUIRES *time for prep*

We eat these for breakfast, lunch, and dinner because it's such a diverse and easy recipe. They're particularly good with my Miso and Turmeric Chickpea Scramble (page 43), some greens, and other raw or cooked seasonal vegetables. The little flecks of sesame seeds look especially beautiful around the lacy edges of the crepe.

Making crepes takes a little bit of practice, and I find the twenty-dollar investment in a basic crepe pan to be worthwhile. This batter is nice and stretchy, and it's hard to mess up if you lay it into the pan a little too thick. If you grease your pan properly each time you start making a new crepe, you should be golden.

⅔ cup (150 mL) chickpea flour

⅔ cup (150 mL) buckwheat flour

2 green onions, finely sliced

2 teaspoons (10 mL) fine sea salt

1 teaspoon (5 mL) chili powder

1-inch (2.5 cm) piece of fresh ginger, peeled and finely grated

1 tablespoon (15 mL) sesame seeds

1½ cups (375 mL) filtered water

canola oil spray, for cooking

1. Preheat the oven to 275°F (140°C). Place a baking sheet in the oven.

2. In a large bowl, combine the chickpea flour, buckwheat flour, sliced green onions, sea salt, chili powder, grated ginger, and sesame seeds. Whisk to combine.

3. Add the filtered water to the flour mixture. Whisk the batter until all flour is incorporated. The batter should be thinner than pancake batter, dripping slowly from the edge of a spoon or spatula, but not as thin as almond milk. Add extra water, by the tablespoon, if necessary.

4. Cover the bowl with plastic wrap and allow the batter to rest for 30 minutes.

5. Heat a crepe pan over medium-high heat. If your batter has thickened and seems almost elastic when you drag a spoon through it, add a couple of tablespoons of water and lightly whisk the batter one more time.

6. Spray the hot crepe pan with canola oil. Ladle about ⅓ cup (75 mL) of batter into the crepe pan. Holding the pan's handle with your non-ladling hand, quickly use your wrist to shake the pan in a circular motion, distributing the crepe batter into a thin, circular crepe. I lift the pan right off the stove and shake it in the air to get the batter moving.

7. Once the crepe appears dry on the surface and some holes have poked through, flip the crepe over. Cook the crepe another 45 seconds, or until lightly browned and dry on the other side.

8. Keep the cooked crepes warm on the baking sheet in the oven while you repeat this process with the remaining batter.

Miso and Turmeric Chickpea Scramble

SERVES *2 to 4*   FREE OF 🌿 🥜 🍚

We eat this vegan scramble on my Savory Ginger Green Onion Crepes (page 40), alongside the Old Reliable Avocado Toast (page 62), or with some Tempeh Bacon (page 47) and roasted potatoes. With the golden hue of the turmeric, the scramble makes a comfortingly familiar impression on the breakfast plate. If you can find some black lava salt, I highly recommend using it in this recipe. The slightly sulfuric flavor of the salt gives this scramble a lightly eggy flavor that really pushes it over the edge. It tastes just as good with regular sea salt and lots of black pepper though. I use green onions in this, but any chopped leafy herbs taste great in addition to the onions.

3 cups (750 mL) cooked chickpeas

1 teaspoon (5 mL) virgin olive oil

2 green onions, finely sliced

½ teaspoon (2 mL) ground turmeric

1 clove garlic, minced

¼ cup (50 mL) chickpea flour

3 tablespoons (45 mL) vegetable stock OR water, plus extra (if necessary)

2 teaspoons (10 mL) mellow or light miso

salt and pepper, to taste

1. Place the cooked chickpeas in a medium bowl, and mash them with a fork. You're looking for a chunky texture with some pieces of chickpea still intact. Set aside.

2. Heat the olive oil in a sauté pan over medium heat. Add the green onions and mashed chickpeas to the pan and stir. Add the turmeric and stir again. Once the scramble is evenly hot, add the garlic and sauté until fragrant, about 30 seconds.

3. Sprinkle the chickpea flour over the scramble in the pan and stir. In a small bowl, lightly whisk together the vegetable stock and miso, just to break up any large lumps of miso. Add this mixture to the pan and stir.

4. Season the scramble with salt and pepper. If the scramble appears dry, add an extra splash of vegetable stock. Once you have the scramble at an ideal point of moistness and the dish is hot all the way through, serve immediately.

Eggplant Bacon

SERVES *4 as a side*   FREE OF 🌿 🥜 🍤   REQUIRES *time for prep*

When you think about eggplant's lush, meaty texture, this preparation seems like a natural progression. The flesh is quite absorbent, so it takes on the smoky-sweet lacquer here quite well. I prefer using this plant-based bacon for a BLT-style set-up (as opposed to my Tempeh Bacon on page 47) because it's naturally lighter and doesn't steal the show from the other sandwich ingredients.

I leave the peel on for that distinctive chew and also because it helps hold the strips together. When you're getting toward the end of the baking time, it's important to keep an eye on the eggplant. It can go from perfect doneness to totally burned in seconds.

1. Preheat the oven to 400°F (200°C). Set a cooling rack on top of a parchment-lined baking sheet.

2. Cut off both ends of the eggplant. Then, with the cut bottom end flat on the cutting board, cut the eggplant down the middle. Lay each half, cut side down, on the board, and slice into ¼-inch (5 mm) strips.

3. In a large colander, layer the eggplant strips, sprinkling liberally with sea salt as you go. After you finish the layering, let the eggplant sit for 15 minutes. I usually set the colander over a plate or in the sink to collect the liquid escaping the eggplant.

4. Rinse the eggplant thoroughly. Towel-dry the pieces of eggplant, and arrange them on the rack-fitted baking sheet.

5. In a small bowl, whisk together the olive oil, maple syrup, apple cider vinegar, smoked paprika, tamari, and miso. Brush half of this mixture onto the eggplant strips. Season the eggplant with black pepper.

6. Slide the baking sheet into the oven and roast for 20 minutes. Remove the eggplant and use tongs to carefully flip over all the strips. Brush the remaining half of the oil and maple syrup mixture onto the exposed side of the eggplant. Season the eggplant with black pepper once more. Roast the eggplant for another 15 minutes or until you start seeing some crisped edges. Serve eggplant bacon hot.

1 large eggplant

1 tablespoon (15 mL) sea salt

1 tablespoon (15 mL) virgin olive oil

1 tablespoon (15 mL) pure maple syrup

1 tablespoon (15 mL) apple cider vinegar

1 teaspoon (5 mL) smoked paprika

½ teaspoon (2 mL) gluten-free tamari soy sauce

½ teaspoon (2 mL) mellow or light miso

freshly ground black pepper, to taste

Tempeh Bacon

SERVES *4 to 6*   FREE OF 🌿 ⬮ ❋   REQUIRES *time for prep*

This is the vegan bacon I serve with a full brunch spread. No one's going to believe that it's real bacon, but it fills the craving for something salty and meaty almost perfectly (without the grease coma afterward). A big plate with a few strips of this tempeh, some toast, Miso and Turmeric Chickpea Scramble (page 43) or Maple Baked Beans (page 48), potatoes, and a pot of coffee spells comfort on a lazy morning, but I eat this with simple rice and vegetable bowls for supper too.

If I'm marinating tempeh (as I am with this recipe), I always try to steam it first to open up its "pores" and make it more receptive to any flavors I want to apply. If you're in a hurry, you can skip that step, but be aware that tempeh's naturally earthy flavor will shine through even more if you do.

1 block (8 ounces/227 g) tempeh, sliced widthwise into ½-inch (1 cm) pieces

2 tablespoons (30 mL) liquid refined coconut oil

1 tablespoon (15 mL) gluten-free tamari soy sauce

1 tablespoon (15 mL) apple cider vinegar

1 tablespoon (15 mL) pure maple syrup

2 teaspoons (10 mL) smoked paprika

½ teaspoon (2 mL) garlic powder

salt and pepper, to taste

1. Preheat the oven to 350°F (180°C). Line a baking sheet with parchment paper and set aside.

2. Place a large pot with an inch (2.5 cm) or so of water onto the stove over medium-low heat. Bring it to a simmer. Transfer the tempeh slices to a steamer basket and place into the pot. Cover the pot with a lid and steam the tempeh for 10 minutes.

3. In a small bowl, whisk together the coconut oil, tamari, apple cider vinegar, maple syrup, smoked paprika, garlic powder, salt, and pepper. This is the tempeh marinade.

4. Remove the tempeh from the steamer and carefully transfer it to a baking dish. Arrange the tempeh slices in a single layer. Pour the marinade over the tempeh slices, spreading them out if necessary. Let the tempeh marinate for at least 20 minutes (or covered overnight in the refrigerator).

5. Arrange the tempeh slices on the parchment-lined baking sheet. Slide the baking sheet into the oven and bake for 25 to 30 minutes, flipping the tempeh pieces over at the halfway point. The edges of the tempeh should be browned and slightly crisp. Serve hot.

Maple Baked Beans

SERVES *8 to 10*   FREE OF 🌿 🥜 💧 🐟   REQUIRES *time to soak and for prep*

This recipe requires some forethought and planning, but it's worth it and you'll have enough beans for days. They take on so much flavor from such a small selection of pantry ingredients, so I find myself making them often in the cold months to heat up on top of thick slices of sourdough toast. These beans do have maple syrup as the title suggests, but I also employ the sticky, gooey nature of Medjool dates to give them that barbecued beans feel that is so satisfying.

1. Place the drained beans in a large, ovenproof, heavy-bottomed soup pot. Cover the beans with the water. Place the pot over medium heat and bring to a boil. Lower the heat to a simmer and cook the beans until just tender, about 40 minutes.

2. Preheat the oven to 325°F (160°C).

3. Reserve 2 cups (500 mL) of the bean cooking water. Drain the beans and return them to the pot. To the beans, add the chopped onion, maple syrup, chopped dates, tomato paste, molasses, apple cider vinegar, mustard, smoked paprika, salt, pepper, and reserved bean cooking water. Give everything a stir to combine.

4. Cover the pot with a tight-fitting lid and put the pot in the oven. Bake the beans until very tender and slightly saucy, about 2 hours. I recommend checking the beans every half hour or so. Add more water and stir if beans seems dry.

5. Serve beans hot with toast or other accompaniments.

1 pound (454 g) dried navy beans, soaked overnight and drained

9 cups (2.25 L) filtered water

1 medium sweet onion, chopped (about 1 cup/250 mL chopped onion)

½ cup (125 mL) pure maple syrup

½ cup (125 mL) Medjool dates, pitted and chopped

¼ cup (50 mL) tomato paste

¼ cup (50 mL) unsulfured molasses

¼ cup (50 mL) apple cider vinegar

1 tablespoon (15 mL) grainy mustard

2 teaspoons (10 mL) smoked paprika

salt and pepper, to taste

FOR SERVING

toast

other accompaniments of your choice

Red Flannel Beet Hash *with* Dill

SERVES *4 to 6*   FREE OF 🌿 🥜 🍚

Crispy potatoes are a familiar and easy vegan component of any breakfast spread, but the addition of beets, avocado, and dill makes these a touch more special. As the beets boil with the potatoes, they stain the white flesh hot pink. You could use purple potatoes for more of a blue flannel approach if you like.

1. Place the chopped potatoes and beets into a large saucepan or braiser-style pot. Cover the vegetables with cold water by 1 inch (2.5 cm). Add the apple cider vinegar. Bring to a boil over medium-high heat. Lower the heat to a simmer and cook until the potatoes are tender and the beets are just tender, about 20 minutes. Drain the vegetables and set aside.

2. Heat the olive oil in a large skillet over medium heat. Add the onions and cook until lightly soft, about 3 minutes. Add the coriander, salt, and pepper and stir until fragrant, about 30 seconds.

3. Add the drained potatoes and beets to the skillet and spread them out in a single layer. Let sit for 5 minutes before stirring. Flip and stir the hash every 5 minutes. Cook the hash for 20 minutes, or until the edges of the potatoes begin to crisp.

4. Lightly toss the hash with the green onions and dill. Serve the hash hot with chopped avocado on top.

2 medium Yukon gold potatoes (generous 1 pound/454 g), chopped into 1-inch (2.5 cm) pieces

2 medium beets (½ pound/227 g), peeled and chopped into ½-inch (1 cm) pieces

1 tablespoon (15 mL) apple cider vinegar

2 tablespoons (30 mL) virgin olive oil

1 medium cooking onion, diced (about 1 cup/250 mL diced onion)

1 teaspoon (5 mL) ground coriander

Salt and pepper, to taste

2 green onions, thinly sliced

¼ cup (50 mL) lightly packed chopped fresh dill (about 3 sprigs)

½ ripe avocado, peeled, pitted and chopped

Toasty French Toast Bake

SERVES *4 to 6* FREE OF 🌾

This is a perfect brunch main for a crowd. You just assemble, bake, and wait for the compliments to roll in. I serve this on the simple side with fresh fruit and maple syrup, but you could smear some jam in between the bread slices before you bake the dish or even sprinkle some chopped pieces of dark chocolate between the layers. I aim for crispy, toasty edges with this, so a finishing touch of maple syrup before the bake goes under the broiler for a minute seems necessary. If you use coconut milk for your base, this bake goes into a more indulgent, bread pudding-like territory.

1. Preheat the oven to 350°F (180°C). Lightly grease an 8-inch (2 L) ovenproof dish with coconut oil.

2. In a medium bowl, whisk together the almond milk, ¼ cup (50 mL) of maple syrup, orange zest, orange juice, vanilla, cinnamon, and arrowroot powder. Keep whisking until combined and there are no dry traces of arrowroot in the mix.

3. Arrange the bread slices in your dish. You can do two flat layers of bread or you can fan them out like a tian (like the one in the accompanying photo). You may have to cut your bread slices in half to accomplish this. Press the bread into the dish.

4. Pour about half the almond milk mixture over the bread. Push the bread down to absorb some of the liquid. Pour the remaining half of the almond milk mixture over the bread. Press down on the bread once more. Let the bread soak in the liquid for 10 minutes.

5. Slide the French toast bake into the oven, and bake until lightly browned on top and much of the liquid has been absorbed, about 30 minutes. Remove the bake from the oven and set the broiler to high. Drizzle the 1 tablespoon (15 mL) of maple syrup over the top of the bake, and slide the dish back into the oven. Broil until the maple syrup caramelizes on the surface of the bread, about 30 seconds.

6. Serve the French toast bake hot with coconut flakes, fruit, berries, and maple syrup.

virgin coconut oil, for greasing the pan

1½ cups (375 mL) unsweetened almond milk OR coconut milk for a richer option

¼ cup + 1 tablespoon (50 mL + 15 mL) pure maple syrup, divided

2 teaspoons (10 mL) orange zest

3 tablespoons (45 mL) fresh orange juice

2 teaspoons (10 mL) pure vanilla extract

1 teaspoon (5 mL) ground cinnamon

2 tablespoons (30 mL) arrowroot powder

12 to 14 1-inch (2.5 cm) slices of stale, whole-grain bread (to fill pan)

FOR SERVING
unsweetened coconut flakes
sliced fresh fruit or whole berries
pure maple syrup

Hemp and Vanilla Bircher Breakfast

SERVES *1*   FREE OF 🌾 🌿   REQUIRES *time for prep*

This is my summer breakfast of choice, served alongside whatever fresh, local fruit is in season. I like a plain chia pudding as well, but the oats and hemp make for a more satisfying morning meal. The mild nuttiness of the hemp seeds bolsters the protein content and improves the creaminess of the mixture. The vanilla really sings when mixed up with some juicy fruit and a dab of nut butter on top, so don't be shy with the toppings.

I like to stir the maple syrup into the bircher in the morning because I find the sweetness fades if thrown into the mix overnight. It packs up tidily in a glass jar, so it's perfect for anyone on the go.

1. In a small sealable jar (or other container), combine the oats, hemp seeds, chia seeds, vanilla powder, sea salt, and almond milk. Stir to combine. Place the lid on the container, and refrigerate for at least 4 hours but ideally overnight.

2. Retrieve and uncover the bircher breakfast after it has chilled. Add the maple syrup to the jar and give it a stir to combine. Serve with fresh fruit and a spoonful of nut or seed butter if you like.

⅓ cup (75 mL) certified gluten-free rolled oats (not instant oats)

1 tablespoon (15 mL) hulled hemp seeds

1 tablespoon (15 mL) chia seeds

¼ teaspoon (1 mL) vanilla powder OR pure vanilla extract

⅛ teaspoon (0.5 mL) fine sea salt

1 cup (250 mL) unsweetened almond milk

1 teaspoon (5 mL) pure maple syrup, or to taste

FOR SERVING

chopped fresh fruit

nut or seed butter

Lazy Steel-Cut Oatmeal

SERVES *1*   FREE OF 🌾 🥜   REQUIRES *time to soak*

This is one of my favorite ways to wake up because I've done almost all of the work the night before. I love the chewy and nutty qualities of steel-cut oats but rarely have the patience to wait the 25 minutes for them to cook on a weekday morning. I simply boil the oats the night before and cover them. With only a twist of the stove knob and a couple of stirs, I get perfect oats in minutes the next morning.

I was turned on to this overnight method when I worked for a local foods café that would serve steel-cut oat porridge in the early mornings. They would bring a massive pot of it to a boil, turn off the heat, and then allow the porridge to cool. Servings would be portioned out and reheated with milk as they were ordered. Brilliant! Toasting the oats in cinnamon-spiked coconut oil gives them a warm spice edge and a touch of creaminess, but you can skip that part if you're feeling truly lazy.

1 teaspoon (5 mL) virgin coconut oil

½ teaspoon (2 mL) ground cinnamon

¼ cup (50 mL) certified gluten-free steel-cut oats

2 tablespoons (30 mL) dried sour cherries or other dried fruit

⅛ teaspoon (0.5 mL) fine sea salt

1 cup (250 mL) unsweetened almond milk, plus extra for reheating, if necessary

1 tablespoon (15 mL) pure maple syrup, or to taste

chopped fresh fruit, for serving (optional)

1. Heat the coconut oil in a small saucepan over medium heat. Add the cinnamon and stir until fragrant, about 30 seconds. Add the oats and stir to coat them in the cinnamon oil. Add the dried cherries, sea salt, and almond milk, and stir.

2. Bring to a boil. After it boils, turn off the heat, remove the saucepan from the burner, and cover with a lid. Leave the oats on the cold stove overnight.

3. The next morning, place the saucepan back on the burner over medium heat. Add more almond milk if you like. When the porridge starts to boil, remove from the heat and scrape it into your serving bowl. Top the porridge with the maple syrup and chopped fruit, if using.

Mega Clump Granola

MAKES *8 to 9 cups (2 to 2.25 L)*   FREE OF 🌿 🌾

Granola was my inaugural DIY food moment. I enjoyed it for the first time at a hippie nature resort in Costa Rica as a teenager, served warm with milk, sliced mango, and fresh juice on the side. That breakfast was one of my main takeaways from the trip. When I returned home, I knew I had to figure out how to recreate it myself. I hadn't cooked much on my own at that point, so that first golden brown batch felt like a huge accomplishment.

Nowadays, I like my granola to border on granola bar territory (lots of clumps!), so this preparation really makes my day. The combination of liquid and dry sweetener along with some ground flax makes the big crunchy shards possible. You pack the mixture down as tight as you can and basically leave it in the oven until golden brown, which is preferable to the messy flipping and stirring methods of most granolas. I toast the oats before mixing them up with the sweetener and spices for an extra depth of flavor. This stuff never lasts long in our house.

5 cups (1.25 L) certified gluten-free rolled oats (not quick-cooking oats)

½ cup (125 mL) pure maple syrup

½ cup (125 mL) maple sugar OR coconut palm sugar

⅔ cup (150 mL) liquid virgin coconut oil

1 tablespoon (15 mL) pure vanilla extract

2 teaspoons (10 mL) ground cinnamon

¾ teaspoon (3 mL) fine sea salt

1 cup (250 mL) raw almonds

1 cup (250 mL) raw sunflower seeds

1 cup (250 mL) raw pumpkin seeds

¼ cup (50 mL) ground flaxseed

1. Preheat the oven to 350°F (180°C). Line a baking sheet (ideally a half-sheet pan with a 1-inch/2.5cm rim) with parchment paper.

2. Spread the oats out on the baking sheet and slide into the oven to toast for about 15 minutes or until fragrant. Remove from the oven and allow to cool.

3. Lower the oven temperature to 325°F (160°C).

4. In a large bowl, whisk together the maple syrup, maple sugar, coconut oil, vanilla, cinnamon, and sea salt. To the maple mixture, add the toasted oats, almonds, sunflower seeds, pumpkin seeds, and ground flaxseed. Stir together until completely combined.

5. Dump the granola mix onto your baking sheet. Spread it out into the corners of the pan. Then, press down on the granola to really compact it together on the baking sheet, almost as if you were making granola bars.

6. Once you have the granola evenly pressed and compacted, slide the baking sheet into the oven. Bake the granola for 40 minutes, rotating the baking sheet halfway through. The granola should be golden brown and firm to the touch. Let the granola cool completely before extracting it from the baking sheet in chunks and breaking it up for storage.

7. The granola will keep in a sealed container in the cupboard for up to 2 weeks.

Plant-Powered Protein Pancakes

SERVES *2*   FREE OF 🌾 🥜 🌰

There are a lot of protein pancake recipes out there and I've tried a bunch of them. I like this version the most because it doesn't rely on powder for the protein content, which I find distracting in a textural sense. This version is just a bunch of naturally plant-powerful ingredients blended with some vanilla, spice, and other pantry stuffs. The temperature is really important for slowly cooking the pancake all the way through, so don't try to rush it. The pancake tastes best with fruit, nut or seed butter, and other goodies on top. Go wild!

1. Place the rolled oats, buckwheat groats, chia seeds, and hemp seeds in a high-speed blender. Cover with the boiling water. Place the lid on the blender and let the mixture sit for 5 minutes.

2. Set a medium sauté pan over medium-low heat.

3. After 5 minutes, add the applesauce, baking powder, vanilla, sea salt, and maple syrup to the blender. Whiz the blender on high until you have a relatively smooth, pancake-like batter. You'll still see little flecks of chia and this is okay.

4. Lightly oil the sauté pan and pour in half the pancake batter. Spread the batter with a spatula. Let the pancake cook for a good 2 minutes on one side, or until the edges of the pancake are dry and the underside is quite browned. Carefully flip the pancake over and cook for another full minute. Repeat this process with the remaining half of the batter.

5. Serve the pancakes with fresh fruit, nut or seed butter, and maple syrup if you like.

¼ cup (50 mL) certified gluten-free rolled oats (not quick-cooking oats)

¼ cup (50 mL) raw buckwheat groats

2 tablespoons (30 mL) chia seeds

2 tablespoons (30 mL) hulled hemp seeds

1 cup (250 mL) boiling water

¼ cup (50 mL) unsweetened applesauce

½ teaspoon (2 mL) aluminum-free baking powder

¼ teaspoon (1 mL) pure vanilla extract

¼ teaspoon (1 mL) sea salt

2 teaspoons (10 mL) pure maple syrup, or to taste

virgin coconut oil, for cooking

FOR SERVING

chopped fresh fruit

nut or seed butter

pure maple syrup

Old Reliable Avocado Toast

SERVES *1*   FREE OF 🥜 💧 🍞

I know that avocado toast combinations and recipes are as plentiful as the day is long, but I stand by this one right here for plenty of reasons. This is also my most frequently made "recipe" of all time, so it felt appropriate to include here.

I prefer the fork-mashing method as opposed to the slice-and-top version of avocado toast, which is admittedly a lot prettier. The mashing allows for proper and even seasoning of the avocado while also creating perfect little divots or "tracks" for the balsamic vinegar to flow in without dripping off of the toast. Old Bay is my go-to spice mix, but if you can't find it where you live, half the amount of celery salt will work.

1. Toast the bread to your preferred level of doneness.

2. Place the toast on a plate. Fan out half of the avocado slices on each piece of toast. Using a fork, mash the avocado into the toast. Sprinkle the toast with the Old Bay seasoning, nutritional yeast, salt, and pepper. Mash the avocado with the fork again, distributing the seasonings evenly.

3. Carefully drizzle the balsamic vinegar on top of the avocado. Top the toast with the hemp seeds and eat immediately.

2 slices sprouted whole-grain bread (gluten-free if required)

½ ripe avocado, pitted and sliced

½ teaspoon (2 mL) Old Bay seasoning

1 teaspoon (5 mL) nutritional yeast

salt and pepper, to taste

1½ teaspoons (7 mL) good-quality balsamic vinegar

2 teaspoons (10 mL) hulled hemp seeds

Soups
&
Stews

The world of soup and stew was the first thing I wanted to take on when I was learning how to cook from a plant-based perspective. These pots of goodness are the perfect vehicles for seasonal vegetables, things in the refrigerator that need to be used up, and economical, deeply nutritious staples like beans, legumes, and whole grains. All the comforting notions of feeling better, being warmed to the core, and knowing that you're cared for are synonymous with this culinary staple. I've learned how to make a few that suit most of my cravings and this section contains the tried and true. Everything from nourishing and quick purées and delicious broth to hearty stews that do well with a crust of bread for scooping is represented here.

Vegetable Stock

MAKES *7 to 8 cups (1.75 to 2 L)*   FREE OF

I buy vegetable stock only out of desperation, when I *really* don't have time. Nothing compares to the flavor of one you make yourself, especially if you adopt my method of slowly browning the vegetables in the pan before adding water. I don't think stock should be made from scraps or garbage bits, since it becomes the foundation of many meals. I always have these ingredients on hand so that if I'm in the kitchen cooking for most of the day, I can have a pot of stock going in the background.

1. Heat the olive oil in a large stock or soup pot over medium heat. Add the onions and sauté until you start to see deep brown marks on some of the sides, about 7 to 8 minutes. Add the carrots and parsnip, and sauté another 4 to 5 minutes, or until the edges are a bit softer. Add the celery and stir.

2. Run the split leek under water to remove any grit, then chop it roughly and add it to the pot along with the garlic cloves. Stir the vegetables until the leeks are bright green and soft, about 4 minutes. Add the thyme sprigs, parsley stems, bay leaves, and black peppercorns to the pot, and stir. Add a good splash of water to the pot, and loosen up some of the brown bits on the bottom with a wooden spoon.

3. Slowly pour the filtered water over the vegetables. Raise the heat to medium-high and cover the pot. Bring to a boil, remove the lid, and then simmer the vegetable stock for about 40 minutes.

4. Allow the vegetable stock to cool slightly before straining and storing in containers. Stock will keep in a sealed container in the refrigerator for 5 to 6 days and in the freezer for 6 months.

1 tablespoon (15 mL) virgin olive oil

2 medium yellow onions, chopped (with papery skin left on)

2 medium carrots, scrubbed and chopped

1 parsnip, chopped

2 stalks celery, scrubbed and chopped

1 large leek, cut down the middle lengthwise

4 cloves garlic, each cut in half

6 sprigs fresh thyme

4 fresh parsley stems (remove leaves)

2 bay leaves

7 whole black peppercorns

8 cups (2 L) filtered water

Cozy Lentil Soup

SERVES *10* FREE OF 🌿 🥜 🍚

I learned how to make lentil soup pretty much the week I decided to go vegan. It's a cheap and comforting protein-rich meal that only gets better as the days go on and it "marinates" in the fridge. I cook the onions for a long time so that they kind of melt into the lentils, making for a rich texture. The first cold fall day that calls for a sweater always has me craving this soup. Out of all the things in this book to make, I would recommend this one the most.

1. In a large, heavy-bottomed pot, heat the olive oil over medium heat. Add the onions to the pot and stir. They should be sizzling but just barely. Continue to stir and sauté the onions until they are completely soft and starting to break down a bit, about 8 minutes.

2. To the onions, add the minced thyme, smoked paprika, and dried tarragon. Stir the spices in and cook until fragrant, about 1 minute.

3. Add the carrots and celery to the pot and stir. Season the whole thing with salt and pepper. Sauté the carrots and celery until barely softened, about 2 minutes. Add the garlic and stir until fragrant, about 30 seconds.

4. Add the lentils to the pot and stir to coat them in the oil, spices, and vegetables. Add the crushed tomatoes and diced tomatoes to the pot and stir to combine. Add the vegetable stock and stir once more.

5. Cover the soup and bring to a boil. Reduce the heat to a simmer and adjust the pot lid slightly, allowing some steam to escape. It should be sitting on top of the pot but slightly askew.

6. Simmer until the lentils are tender, stirring occasionally, about 25 minutes. Check the soup for seasoning, adjust accordingly, and serve hot.

3 tablespoons (45 mL) virgin olive oil

1 medium yellow onion, small dice

2 teaspoons (10 mL) minced fresh thyme leaves (about 4 sprigs)

½ teaspoon (2 mL) smoked paprika

½ teaspoon (2 mL) dried tarragon

2 medium carrots, small dice

2 stalks celery, small dice

salt and pepper, to taste

4 cloves garlic, minced

1 cup (250 mL) French lentils, rinsed

1 can (14 ounces/398 mL) crushed tomatoes (I prefer fire-roasted)

1 can (14 ounces/398 mL) diced tomatoes (I prefer fire-roasted)

6 cups (1.5 L) vegetable stock

Weeknight Root Vegetable Dal

SERVES *4*   FREE OF 🌿 🥜 🍚

This thin and fragrant lentil stew recipe was quite popular with my recipe testers. A bunch of them told me they had already started working it into their weeknight dinner rotation. With the "throw it all in the pot" preparation method, I totally understand why. I'm usually skeptical of one-pot dinners that don't coax the flavor out of the aromatics, but in this context it totally works.

1. To a medium soup pot, add the rinsed lentils, diced root vegetables, diced onion, tomatoes, garlic, ginger, turmeric, and chili flakes. Pour the water into the pot and give everything a little stir.

2. Place the pot on the stove over medium heat. Bring to a boil and then simmer for about 40 minutes, whisking the dal often. Toward the end, the lentils should be completely broken down. In the last 10 minutes of cooking, whisk the dal vigorously to encourage the breaking down of the lentils. It should appear quite soupy. Season the dal generously with salt and pepper. Keep warm.

3. Heat the coconut oil in a small sauté pan over medium-high heat. Add the cumin seeds, coriander seeds, and mustard seeds. Once the seeds are fragrant and popping, remove from the heat.

4. Gently spoon the toasted spice oil (with the whole spices) on top of the dal. You can lightly stir it in if you like. You can also portion the dal out first and then spoon the spice oil on top if you like. Garnish the dal with the chopped cilantro. Serve the dal hot with lemon wedges.

1 cup (250 mL) red split lentils, rinsed

1 cup (250 mL) finely diced root vegetables of your choice, such as carrots, celery root, and beets

1 small yellow onion, finely diced

1 cup (250 mL) cherry or grape tomatoes, halved

4 cloves garlic, minced

2-inch (5 cm) piece of fresh ginger, peeled and minced

1 teaspoon (5 mL) ground turmeric

pinch of dried chili flakes

3½ cups (875 mL) filtered water

salt and pepper, to taste

2 tablespoons (30 mL) virgin coconut oil

½ teaspoon (2 mL) cumin seeds

½ teaspoon (2 mL) coriander seeds

½ teaspoon (2 mL) mustard seeds

⅓ cup (75 mL) chopped fresh cilantro leaves, for garnish

lemon wedges, for serving

Leaf and Stem Green Tortilla Soup

SERVES *4 to 5*   FREE OF

This soup is so comforting. It has the creaminess from the blended tortillas, the zippy flavors of salsa verde, and textural garnishes galore. As a bonus, it's a great way to use up the often-neglected stems of greens. I usually use stems when I make fresh juice, but this soup is a warm, substantial, and visually appealing change of pace from that.

1. Place the top oven rack about 3 to 4 inches (7.5 to 10 cm) from the broiler. Preheat the broiler to high. Place the peeled tomatillos on a baking sheet and slide the baking sheet into the oven. Broil the tomatillos for 8 to 10 minutes or until lightly blackened and slightly oozing. Set the broiled tomatillos aside to cool.

2. Lower the oven temperature to 400°F (200°C). Cut the tortillas into strips and lay them on a baking sheet. Toss the tortilla strips with 1 tablespoon (15 mL) of the sunflower oil and some salt, to taste. After the strips are evenly coated, arrange them in a single layer, and slide the baking sheet into the oven. Bake until the tortilla strips are lightly browned and crisp, about 15 minutes. Remove from oven and set aside.

3. Heat the remaining 1 tablespoon (15 mL) of the sunflower oil in a large pot over medium heat. Add the white onions to the pot and sauté until soft and translucent, about 4 minutes. Add the garlic, jalapeño, cumin, and coriander. Stir for about 30 seconds or until the garlic is very fragrant.

4. Add the broiled tomatillos and vegetable stock to the pot. Bring to a boil. Add ⅓ of the baked tortilla strips and all the chopped greens and their stems. Cook until the greens are vibrant green, about 1 minute. Remove from the heat.

5. With a blender, purée the soup in batches until totally smooth. Once all the soup is puréed, return it to the pot and bring it back to a boil on the stove. Season the soup with salt and pepper.

6. Serve the soup hot and garnished with the remaining baked tortilla strips, diced avocado, chopped cilantro, and lime wedges on the side.

¾ pound (341 g) fresh tomatillos, papery skins removed

8 small (6-inch/15 cm) corn tortillas

2 tablespoons (30 mL) sunflower oil, divided

1 medium white onion, chopped

4 cloves garlic, chopped

1 jalapeño pepper, seeded and chopped

2 teaspoons (10 mL) ground cumin

2 teaspoons (10 mL) ground coriander

5 cups (1.25 L) vegetable stock

3 cups (750 mL) chopped greens with stems, such as kale, collards, and spinach

salt and pepper, to taste

FOR SERVING

tortilla strips

diced ripe avocado

chopped fresh cilantro leaves

lime wedges

Creamy Jalapeño Corn Chowder

SERVES *4*   FREE OF 🌿 🥜 🍚

My dad grows the best corn on the planet in the summertime and drops it off at my door every week before he heads to work (usually along with a bunch of other goodies from his garden). The seed catalogue that he orders from has a "Customer Favorite!" badge next to this variety of corn, and he's convinced that this is due to his endorsement over the years. I honestly wouldn't be surprised. The corn is so sweet, tender, and creamy. It's perfect on its own with a sprinkle of salt but even better in this chowder with jalapeño, Old Bay seasoning, and creamy Yukon gold potatoes. I freeze a bunch of summer corn before it's gone so that I can make this thick and delicious soup all winter.

2 teaspoons (10 mL) virgin olive oil

1 medium yellow onion, small dice

1 stalk celery, small dice

1 small red bell pepper, small dice

2 teaspoons (10 mL) minced fresh thyme leaves (about 4 sprigs)

½ teaspoon (2 mL) smoked paprika

½ teaspoon (2 mL) Old Bay seasoning OR celery salt

1 jalapeño pepper, seeded and minced

1 clove garlic, minced

1 pound (454 g) new potatoes, diced

3 cups (750 mL) fresh OR frozen corn kernels (about 4 fresh cobs)

salt and pepper, to taste

4 cups (1 L) vegetable stock

2 teaspoons (10 mL) white wine vinegar

chopped chives, for garnish

1. Heat the olive oil in a large soup pot over medium heat. Add the onions, and sauté until soft and translucent, about 4 minutes.

2. Add the celery and red pepper and stir. Add the thyme, paprika, Old Bay, and jalapeño. Sauté the vegetables and spices until the celery is soft and the spices are fragrant, about 1 minute. Add the garlic and cook until fragrant, 30 seconds.

3. Add the potatoes and corn, and stir to coat in the spices and oil. Season everything generously with salt and pepper. Pour the vegetable stock over the vegetables. Cover and bring to a boil. Lower the heat and simmer until the potatoes are quite tender, about 25 minutes.

4. Carefully ladle half of the soup into a blender. Place the lid on top and slowly bring the speed up to high. Blend until you have a smooth and creamy purée. Add the puréed soup back to the pot and stir to combine into one unified chowder. Add the white wine vinegar and stir once more.

5. Check the soup for seasoning and adjust if necessary. Serve the chowder hot with the chopped chives on top.

Moroccan Stew

SERVES 6   FREE OF 🌿 🥜 🍚

This is a dish that I love to fix in the depths of winter because it makes the kitchen smell exotic and incredible. There's something about using cinnamon in a savory context that is so intoxicating but so simple to execute. I tasted a very similar dish the first time I ate at a higher-end vegan restaurant. A little over a year later, I started interning at that same restaurant as a line cook. Eventually, I learned their secrets to making this comforting, vegetable-packed pot of food. It was all about the slowly stewed onions and spices, sweating every shred of rawness out of both to express their ultimate flavor. My version is a touch more streamlined and features plumped pieces of Medjool dates as well, which are as unexpected as they are lovely.

1. Heat the coconut oil in a large, heavy-bottomed soup pot over medium heat. Add the onions and immediately lower the heat until they are sizzling quietly. When the onions are soft and translucent, add the cinnamon, cumin, coriander, and chili flakes, if using. Slowly sauté and stir the spiced onion mixture until the onions are quite soft, about 5 minutes.

2. Add the garlic and sauté until fragrant, about 30 seconds. Add the chopped dates, carrots, and sweet potatoes. Season the vegetables with salt and pepper. Stir to coat the vegetables in the spices and oil. Add the crushed tomatoes and stir. Add 3 cups (750 mL) of the vegetable stock.

3. Bring to a boil uncovered, and simmer until the sweet potatoes are just tender, about 10 to 12 minutes. Add the yellow peppers and chickpeas and stir. Season the whole thing again with salt and pepper. If the stew seems too thick, add the remaining 1 cup (250 mL) of vegetable stock.

4. Simmer until the yellow peppers are tender and the sweet potatoes are quite soft, about 5 minutes. Check the soup for seasoning and adjust if necessary. Serve the stew hot with a few green olives per portion, lemon wedges, and warm cooked grain.

2 teaspoons (10 mL) virgin coconut oil

1 medium yellow onion, small dice

2 teaspoons (10 mL) ground cinnamon

2 teaspoons (10 mL) ground cumin

2 teaspoons (10 mL) ground coriander

½ teaspoon (2 mL) dried chili flakes (optional)

2 cloves garlic, minced

3 to 4 Medjool dates, pitted and chopped

2 carrots, chopped into ½-inch (1 cm) pieces

1 large sweet potato, peeled and chopped into ½-inch (1 cm) pieces

salt and pepper, to taste

1 can (28 ounces/796 mL) crushed tomatoes (I prefer fire-roasted)

3 to 4 cups (750 mL to 1 L) vegetable stock

1 yellow pepper, stemmed and chopped into ½-inch (1 cm) pieces

2 cups (500 mL) cooked chickpeas

FOR SERVING

pitted green olives

lemon wedges

cooked brown rice, millet, or whole wheat couscous

Creamy Winter Vegetable Stew
with Mustard and Lemon

SERVES *4* FREE OF 🌿 🥜 🍚

Without the use of preserved tomatoes, I was feeling a bit stumped as to what kind of thick, hearty stew I could make that would still satisfy with full flavor. I started thinking about rich chowders and how I could use vegetables and beans. I took all the creamy, winter-white vegetables I could find and stewed them with grainy mustard, lemon, and garlic, and the results were exactly what I was aiming for: filling and rich but still vibrant and light.

1. Heat the olive oil in a large, heavy-bottomed pot over medium heat. Add the diced onions and sauté until soft and translucent, about 4 minutes. Add the leeks and continue to sauté until the leeks are soft, about 4 minutes more. Add the minced garlic and thyme, and cook until fragrant, about 30 seconds, stirring constantly.

2. Add the chopped parsnips, celery root, and cauliflower florets and stir to coat in the oil. Add the grainy mustard, salt and pepper, nutritional yeast, and Old Bay seasoning. Stir to coat the vegetables in the spices. Add the lemon juice and stir.

3. Add the vegetable stock, stir again, cover, and bring to a boil. Once boiling, remove the lid and reduce the heat to a simmer. Let the chowder cook and bubble until the parsnips and celery root pieces are tender, about 15 to 18 minutes.

4. Ladle half of the stew into a blender, and carefully purée until smooth. Pour the puréed portion of stew back into the soup pot. If the stew is too thick, add enough vegetable stock to loosen it up to your liking. Bring the stew back to a boil and serve hot.

1 tablespoon (15 mL) virgin olive oil

1 large cooking onion, small dice (about 1¾ cups/425 mL diced onion)

1 leek, small dice (white and light-green part only)

4 cloves garlic, minced

2 teaspoons (10 mL) minced fresh thyme leaves (about 4 sprigs)

1 medium parsnip, peeled and chopped

½ large or 1 small celery root, peeled and chopped into 1-inch (2.5 cm) pieces (1½ cups/375 mL chopped celery root)

2 cups (500 mL) 1-inch (2.5 cm) cauliflower florets

1½ tablespoons (22 mL) grainy mustard

salt and pepper, to taste

2 teaspoons (10 mL) nutritional yeast

1 teaspoon (5 mL) Old Bay seasoning

¼ cup (50 mL) fresh lemon juice

3½ cups (875 mL) vegetable stock, plus extra if needed

Small-Batch Roasted Soup

SERVES *2* FREE OF 🌿 🥜 🍚

If you have a decent blender, good Vegetable Stock (page 67), and the ability to roast vegetables, you can make a beautiful puréed soup that will rival any restaurant's daily feature. Here, I've used asparagus and fennel, but the possibilities are endless (sweet potatoes and Poblano peppers, parsnips and cauliflower, or butternut squash and apples). For this style of soup, I purée the vegetables with a cup of cooked and drained beans/legumes for creaminess and to round it out as a meal. I used navy beans here, but you could easily use chickpeas, kidney beans, or even brown lentils. A crust of bread on the side or a scoop of rice right on top makes this soup weeknight-easy and so cozy.

1. Preheat the oven to 400°F (200°C).

2. On a baking sheet lined with parchment paper, toss the chopped vegetables, chopped onions, and garlic clove with the olive oil and some salt and pepper. After the vegetables are evenly coated with the oil, slide the baking sheet into the oven.

3. Roast the vegetables until the onions are browned slightly and your seasonal vegetables are softening. Asparagus or broccoli take about 15 to 20 minutes to cook, while sweet potatoes and squash take about 35 minutes to cook. Remove from the oven when done.

4. Place the roasted vegetables in a blender. Add the beans, vegetable stock, and lemon juice. Slowly bring the blender speed up to high, and keep blending until you have a smooth and creamy consistency.

5. Pour the blended soup into a medium saucepan and bring to a boil, uncovered. Check the soup for seasoning and adjust accordingly. Serve soup hot with bread on the side or cooked rice, millet, or quinoa on top.

2 cups (500 mL) chopped seasonal vegetables (I use asparagus and fennel)

1 small onion, chopped

1 clove garlic, peeled

2 teaspoons (10 mL) virgin olive oil

salt and pepper, to taste

1 cup (250 mL) cooked beans (I use navy beans)

1½ cups (375 mL) vegetable stock

2 teaspoons (10 mL) fresh lemon juice

FOR SERVING

bread OR cooked rice, millet, or quinoa

Bloody Caesar Gazpacho

SERVES *4 to 6*   FREE OF 🌿 🥣   REQUIRES *time to soak*

This is my playful take on the popular Canadian brunch drink (very similar to a Bloody Mary). It has all the savory flavor of a Caesar but packaged into a summery lunch course. As with the actual cocktail, garnishes are very important here. Tomato gazpacho always has a V8 vibe to me, so I try to keep some texture within the soup itself and include whole elements on top to distinguish it from vegetable juice.

1. In a large bowl, toss together the chopped tomatoes, red onions, cucumber, celery, garlic, chili, if using, and celery salt. Cover the bowl with plastic wrap, and let it sit at room temperature for 1 hour.

2. Uncover the vegetables and transfer them to the bowl of a food processor. Pour all the marinating liquid from the bowl into the food processor as well. Drain the almonds and add them to the food processor. Run the motor on high until the vegetables and almonds are puréed. Reduce the speed to low, and drizzle in the red wine vinegar and olive oil. Stop the machine when you have a smooth mixture.

3. Run the gazpacho through a fine strainer into a large bowl. Season with vegan Worcestershire sauce, hot sauce, and black pepper.

4. Store the gazpacho, covered, in the refrigerator until ready to serve with the garnishes. The gazpacho will keep in the refrigerator for up to 5 days.

6 cups chopped ripe tomatoes

1 small red onion, chopped

1 English cucumber, chopped

2 stalks celery, chopped

2 cloves garlic, chopped

fresh chili pepper, chopped, to taste (optional)

2 teaspoons (10 mL) celery salt

⅓ cup (75 mL) raw almonds, soaked for at least 6 hours

2 tablespoons (30 mL) red wine vinegar

⅓ cup (75 mL) virgin olive oil

vegan gluten-free Worcestershire sauce OR gluten-free tamari soy sauce, to taste

hot sauce, such as Tabasco, to taste

freshly ground black pepper, to taste

GARNISHES

thinly sliced celery

thinly sliced red onion

lime wedges

pitted green olives

additional hot sauce, such as Tabasco

Tofu Noodle Soup *with* Coconut Lemongrass Broth

SERVES *4 to 6*   FREE OF 🌿 🥜 🍚

This soup has some subtle, aromatic flavors that are just right with a tangle of warm rice noodles and a squeeze of lime over the top. I steep the chopped lemongrass like a tea to form the base of the broth. Herbs, ginger, and coconut milk finish it off and give it a beautiful green hue.

1. In a large pot, bring the vegetable stock and chopped lemongrass to a boil. Remove from the heat and allow the lemongrass to steep for 10 minutes. Strain the steeped broth. Discard the lemongrass.

2. Transfer the broth to a blender. Add the coconut milk, cilantro, salt, and pepper. Blend the mixture on high until completely smooth. Set aside.

3. In the same large pot, heat the coconut oil over medium heat. Add the shallots, chili, and ginger. Stir and sauté until the onions are translucent and slightly soft, about 2 minutes.

4. Add the snow peas and broccoli florets and stir. Season the vegetables with salt and pepper. Add the tofu and stir. Pour the coconut lemongrass broth and tamari into the pot, and stir to combine. Taste the broth for seasoning and adjust if necessary.

5. Bring the soup to a boil. Lower the heat to a simmer and cook, uncovered, until broccoli is tender, about 4 minutes. Stir in the lime juice.

6. Serve the soup hot with cooked rice or rice noodles and lime wedges on the side.

4 cups (1 L) vegetable stock

2 stalks fresh lemongrass, chopped

1 cup (250 mL) full-fat coconut milk

1 cup (250 mL) tightly packed fresh cilantro leaves

salt and pepper, to taste

1 tablespoon (15 mL) virgin coconut oil

1 medium shallot, small dice (about ½ cup/125 mL diced shallot)

1 small green chili pepper, seeded and minced

2-inch (5 cm) piece fresh ginger, peeled and minced

1 cup (250 mL) snow peas

1½ cups (375 mL) small broccoli florets

1 block (14 ounces/398 g) extra-firm tofu, drained and cut into ½-inch (1 cm) cubes

1 teaspoon (5 mL) gluten-free tamari soy sauce

2 tablespoons (30 mL) fresh lime juice

FOR SERVING

cooked rice OR rice noodles

lime wedges

Chipotle Pumpkin Chili *with* Tempeh and Beer

SERVES *4 to 6*   FREE OF 🫛 🌾

I make chili once a year when the weather turns cold, and then I've usually had my fill for a whole year until I make it the following winter. It's a craving that becomes obsessive when I get it, but because my chili recipe is so intensely flavorful (and because it makes a huge pot), it satisfies in one batch. The chipotles in adobo and a spoonful of cocoa powder are my secret weapons here. They make it seem like the chili has been stewing for hours. This recipe is one of the only instances when I don't advise on steaming tempeh ahead of time. The fine chopping helps the protein integrate and mingle with the flavors flawlessly.

1. Heat the olive oil in a large pot over medium heat. Add the onions and sauté until translucent, about 3 minutes.

2. Add the garlic, chipotles, cumin, chili powder, coriander, and cocoa powder to the pot and stir. Keep stirring until the garlic is very fragrant, about 30 seconds. The pot should look quite dry.

3. Pour the beer into the pot, and start scraping up any bits from the bottom. Add the chopped pumpkin, black beans, tempeh, and tomatoes. Stir to combine. Season the chili liberally with salt and pepper. Stir one more time.

4. Cover and bring to a boil. Lower the heat to a simmer. Cook the chili, covered, for 30 to 35 minutes or until the pieces of pumpkin are tender. Stir the chili occasionally.

5. Serve the chili hot with chopped cilantro and diced avocado.

1 tablespoon (15 mL) virgin olive oil

1 large onion, chopped

3 cloves garlic, minced

3 to 5 canned chipotles in adobo, chopped (use more or less, depending on how spicy you want your chili)

2 teaspoons (10 mL) ground cumin

2 teaspoons (10 mL) chili powder

1 teaspoon (5 mL) ground coriander

1 tablespoon (15 mL) unsweetened cocoa powder

1 cup (250 mL) beer (gluten-free if required) OR vegetable stock OR water

2 cups (500 mL) peeled and chopped pumpkin OR butternut squash OR sweet potatoes

2 cups (500 mL) cooked black beans

1 block (8 ounces/227 g) tempeh, finely chopped or crumbled

1 can (28 ounces/796 mL) crushed tomatoes

salt and pepper, to taste

FOR SERVING

chopped fresh cilantro leaves

diced ripe avocado

Sweet and Sour Cabbage Stew
with Rosemary

SERVES *4 to 6*   FREE OF 🌿 🥜 🥛

Cabbage is the unsung hero of winter and this soup is my way of saying thanks for its existence. A cabbage can hang out in the back of your refrigerator for weeks and the rest of this soup is essentially pantry or cellar stock. It's important to make the shreds of cabbage short with this recipe. Slurping up long strands of cabbage can be awkward and especially messy when you're dealing with a deep purple broth.

1. Heat the olive oil in a large pot over medium heat. Add the onions, carrots, and apples, and sauté until the onions are quite soft and translucent, about 4 minutes.

2. Add the rosemary, cumin seeds, caraway seeds, smoked paprika, and nutmeg, and stir. Keep stirring until the spices are quite fragrant, about 30 seconds. Add the cabbage and stir to combine.

3. Add the apple cider vinegar and maple syrup, and stir. Scrape any browned bits from the bottom of the pot. Pour in the vegetable stock and stir.

4. In a piece of cheesecloth or a loose-leaf tea infuser, secure the whole cloves and bay leaf. Drop the sachet into the pot, and submerge it with your spoon. Season the stew with salt and pepper.

5. Bring to a boil. Lower the heat to a simmer and cook the stew, covered, for 45 minutes or until the cabbage is very tender.

6. Serve the stew hot with chopped parsley or dill.

a piece of cheesecloth or a loose-leaf tea infuser

1 tablespoon (15 mL) virgin olive oil

1 large yellow onion, small dice

1 medium carrot, small dice

1 medium sweet apple, peeled and chopped

1½ teaspoons (7 mL) minced fresh rosemary (nearly 2 sprigs)

1 teaspoon (5 mL) cumin seeds

1 teaspoon (5 mL) caraway seeds

1 teaspoon (5 mL) smoked paprika

¼ teaspoon (1 mL) ground nutmeg

1 small red cabbage, finely shredded (about 4 to 5 cups/1 to 1.25 L shredded cabbage)

3 tablespoons (45 mL) apple cider vinegar

2 tablespoons (30 mL) pure maple syrup

4 cups (1 L) vegetable stock

5 whole cloves

1 bay leaf

salt and pepper, to taste

chopped fresh flat-leaf parsley OR fresh dill, for serving

Deep Immune Cup of Soup

SERVES *3 to 4*   FREE OF 🥄 🥣

This soup gets the job done if your head is feeling stuffy. It's very sharp tasting with an ample amount of ginger, garlic, and apple cider vinegar. Turmeric is an anti-inflammatory all-star that I try to consume every day, but its presence is extra functional here. I add orzo pasta to give it that comforting noodle soup feeling, but you could replace it with some extra chopped vegetables or greens. Sometimes I make this up without the pasta and strain it off to sip as a healing broth.

1. Heat the olive oil in a large pot over medium heat. Add the onions, carrots, and celery. Sauté and stir vegetables until the onions are very soft and translucent, about 5 minutes.

2. Add the garlic, ginger, turmeric, and chili flakes, and stir until the spices are fragrant, about 30 seconds. Add the orzo and vegetable stock. Bring to a boil. Lower the heat to a simmer, and cook until pasta is just tender, about 7 minutes.

3. In a small bowl, stir together the miso and apple cider vinegar. Ladle 2 to 3 tablespoons (30 to 45 mL) of the warm broth into the small bowl to fully dissolve the miso. Add this mixture to the soup along with the chopped parsley. Season the soup with salt and pepper at this point if you like. Serve immediately.

1 teaspoon (5 mL) virgin olive oil

1 small yellow onion, diced

1 medium carrot, diced

1 stalk celery, diced

3 cloves garlic, minced

2-inch (5 cm) piece of fresh ginger, peeled and minced

2 teaspoons (10 mL) turmeric powder

½ teaspoon (2 mL) dried chili flakes, or to taste

⅔ cup (150 mL) whole-grain orzo pasta (or other small, shaped pasta)

4 cups (1 L) vegetable stock

2 teaspoons (10 mL) mellow or light miso

1 teaspoon (5 mL) apple cider vinegar

⅓ cup (75 mL) chopped fresh flat-leaf parsley

salt and pepper, to taste

Smoky Saffron Chickpea, Chard, and Rice Soup

SERVES 6   FREE OF 🌿 🥜 🍚

I'm always trying to come up with new ways to combine beans and rice, that classic complete protein combination. A hearty soup is an easy outlet for that, and I load this one up with greens, vegetables, and the mellow, but distinct, flavor of saffron. The lightly smoky broth is pretty much begging to be sopped up with some crusty bread.

1. Heat the olive oil in a large soup pot over medium heat. Add the onions and celery. Stir and sauté until the onions are quite soft and translucent, about 5 minutes.

2. Add the garlic, smoked paprika, and tomato paste, and stir. Add the zucchini, chickpeas, and rice. Season with salt and pepper. Add the saffron and vegetable stock, stir, and cover. Bring to a boil and then reduce the heat to a simmer. Cook, covered, until the rice is just cooked through, about 25 minutes. Add the chopped chard to the pot and continue to cook until it has just wilted, about 3 minutes.

3. Stir in the parsley and lemon juice and serve immediately.

2 teaspoons (10 mL) virgin olive oil

1 medium yellow onion, small dice

1 stalk celery, small dice

3 cloves garlic, minced

1½ teaspoons (7 mL) smoked paprika

¼ cup (50 mL) tomato paste

1 medium zucchini, chopped into ½-inch (1 cm) pieces

1½ cups (375 mL) cooked chickpeas

⅓ cup (75 mL) medium-grain brown rice, rinsed

salt and pepper, to taste

pinch of saffron threads

5 to 6 cups (1.25 to 1.5 L) vegetable stock

1 bunch chard, leaves chopped (about 6 cups/1.5 L chopped chard)

¼ cup (50 mL) chopped fresh flat-leaf parsley

1 tablespoon (15 mL) fresh lemon juice

Salads & Dressings

The association of plant-based eating and constant salads doesn't bother me, because it honestly reflects my real-life eating patterns. I tend to be a big eater, and vegetable-packed salads fit the bill nicely because I can eat them with abandon, all in the name of my health. A thoughtful salad is the most direct and freshest way to use up entirely local produce when it's in season. And if you can make a salad that people crave, you've accomplished a serious feat as a plant-based cook. A shortcut to this accomplishment is a good dressing, and I provide some delicious ones in this chapter. Most of the dressings in this section can be used for alternative recipes and dishes, too. The horseradish dressing for the Caramelized Onion Potato Salad (page 106) is delicious simply drizzled over roasted root vegetables, and the Avocado Citrus Dressing (page 100) is a perfect dip for summer rolls and fresh raw vegetables.

Cider and Sunflower Dressing

MAKES *1¼ cups (300 mL)*   FREE OF 🌿 🥜 🌾

Next to my Old Reliable Avocado Toast (page 62), this is the most frequently made recipe in my house. We drizzle it over salads, yes, but also over rice bowls, roasted vegetables, basically anything that needs a little extra something. This dressing is especially nice if you can find cold-pressed sunflower oil, which has the nutty flavor of toasted sunflower seeds.

1. To a blender, add the apple cider vinegar, lemon juice, water, tamari, Dijon mustard, maple syrup, garlic, salt, and pepper. Blitz the mixture on medium-high speed until creamy.

2. With the blender on low, remove the small feed cap in the middle of the lid. With the blender running, slowly drizzle in the sunflower oil. After you've added all the oil, stop the blender. Place the feed cap back on, and then whiz the dressing on high for a few seconds to fully combine. Store the dressing in the refrigerator for up to 1 week.

¼ cup (50 mL) apple cider vinegar

1 teaspoon (5 mL) fresh lemon juice

2 tablespoons (30 mL) filtered water

¼ teaspoon (1 mL) gluten-free tamari soy sauce

1 teaspoon (5 mL) Dijon mustard

2 teaspoons (10 mL) pure maple syrup

1 clove garlic, chopped

salt and pepper, to taste

¾ cup (175 mL) sunflower oil

Creamy Garlic Dressing

MAKES *1 cup (250 mL)*   FREE OF 🌿 🍚

I keep raw cashew butter on hand almost exclusively for this dressing and any slight variations on it like the dressing used in my Broccoli Caesar with Smoky Tempeh Bits (page 110). It tastes like a creamy mayonnaise-based dressing because of the cashew butter's mellow sweetness and naturally high fat content. For that reason, it works as a great sandwich spread if you're doing a vegan BLT with the Eggplant Bacon (page 44), some fresh lettuce, and a juicy slice of tomato. I love the rousing chorus of "This doesn't have dairy?!" when I serve it to people for the first time.

¼ cup (50 mL) raw cashew butter

¼ cup (50 mL) filtered water

2 cloves garlic, finely grated with a Microplane grater

3 tablespoons (45 mL) fresh lemon juice

2 teaspoons (10 mL) Dijon mustard

¼ cup + 2 tablespoons (50 mL + 30 mL) virgin olive oil

salt and pepper, to taste

1. In a jar with a tight-fitting lid, combine the cashew butter and water. Stir with a spoon or small spatula until the cashew butter is broken up and slightly incorporated. Press the chunks of cashew butter up against the sides of the jar to get it as integrated as possible.

2. Add the garlic, lemon juice, Dijon mustard, olive oil, salt, and pepper. Tightly secure the lid, and shake the jar vigorously until the dressing has a smooth and creamy consistency. Store the dressing in the refrigerator for up to 1 week.

Oil-Free Sundried Tomato and Oregano Dressing

MAKES *3 cups (750 mL)*   FREE OF

Certain occasions call for an oil-free dressing or sauce that can still deliver flavor-wise. I tried something similar to this at a raw food potluck one time and found the rough recipe scribbled on the back of a receipt in my purse months later. I'm so glad I didn't throw that one out! I usually serve this over warm grain bowls with some shaved raw vegetables and a squeeze of lemon to wake up all the flavors. I also love this one with a finely shredded kale salad or other slaw-type recipe.

1. Bring the 2 cups (500 mL) of water to a boil. In a small bowl, combine the sundried tomatoes and boiling water. Let the sundried tomatoes soften for about 10 minutes.

2. Pour the sundried tomatoes and the soaking liquid into a blender. Add the garlic, shallots, Dijon mustard, maple syrup, oregano, salt, and pepper. Whiz the mixture on high until it has a smooth and creamy consistency. This takes a full 3 minutes with a couple of pauses for scraping down. Store the dressing in the refrigerator for up to 1 week.

2 cups (500 mL) filtered water

½ cup (125 mL) sundried tomato halves (not oil-packed)

1 clove garlic, chopped

1 small shallot, chopped (about ¼ cup/50 mL chopped shallots)

2 tablespoons (30 mL) Dijon mustard

2 tablespoons (30 mL) pure maple syrup

¼ teaspoon (1 mL) dried oregano

salt and pepper, to taste

Wedge Salad *with* Avocado Citrus Dressing

SERVES 6   FREE OF 🌿 🥜 🥬

The presentation of this salad is delightfully old-fashioned, but the components of the dressing itself are anything but. Sometimes I'll lightly brush wedges of lettuce and endive with oil and grill them over a medium flame for about a minute, and then treat them to a hearty drizzle of the simultaneously bright and rich avocado dressing. The smoky essence from the grill changes the dynamic of the salad entirely.

1. MAKE THE DRESSING: In a blender, combine the water, orange juice, lemon juice, lime juice, apple cider vinegar, agave nectar, grapeseed oil, jalapeño, avocado, dill, and salt and pepper. Whiz on high until it has a smooth and creamy consistency, about 1 full minute. Set aside.

2. MAKE THE SALAD: Lay the wedges of romaine, radicchio, and Boston or Bibb lettuce out on a platter or divide among individual plates. Season the wedges with salt and pepper. Pour the dressing evenly over the wedges. Finish with the halved cherry tomatoes and chopped dill. Serve immediately.

DRESSING

¼ cup (50 mL) filtered water

3 tablespoons (45 mL) fresh orange juice (from about 1 small orange)

3 tablespoons (45 mL) fresh lemon juice (from about 1 lemon)

2 tablespoons (30 mL) fresh lime juice (from about 1 lime)

1 tablespoon (15 mL) apple cider vinegar

2 tablespoons (30 mL) raw agave nectar

3 tablespoons (45 mL) grapeseed or other neutral-flavored oil

1 small jalapeño pepper, seeded and chopped

1 medium, ripe avocado, peeled and pitted

3 tablespoons (45 mL) chopped fresh dill (about 3 sprigs)

salt and pepper, to taste

SALAD

3 romaine hearts, cut into wedges

1 head radicchio, cut into wedges

1 head Boston or Bibb lettuce, cut into wedges

salt and pepper, to taste

1 pint (2 cups/500 mL) cherry tomatoes, halved

chopped fresh dill, for garnish

Thanksgiving Panzanella Salad
with Delicata Squash

SERVES 6   FREE OF 🥜 🌾

I usually make this dish in the weeks leading up to Thanksgiving, just to get us properly excited for the big meal. It has the satisfying starchy aspect of traditional herbed stuffing or dressing, the sweet squash, some hearty greens, and a tart kiss from the pomegranate seeds. It makes for a dramatic and beautiful presentation if you decide to lay it on the holiday table as well. Of all the squashes, I love delicata the most because it doesn't require peeling and it has a creamy, mild flavor. The skin helps the squash seem a little extra crispy too, which is perfect for this salad.

1. Preheat the oven to 400°F (200°C). Line two baking sheets with parchment paper and set aside.

2. MAKE THE DRESSING: In a medium bowl, whisk together the balsamic vinegar, salt, pepper, minced garlic, Dijon mustard, maple syrup, and olive oil. Set aside.

3. MAKE THE SALAD: Cut the delicata squash down the middle lengthwise. Scoop out the seeds and discard them. Cut the squash halves into ¼-inch (5 mm) slices, and then transfer those slices to one of the parchment-lined baking sheets.

4. Cut the shallots into ½-inch (1 cm) wedges, trying to preserve the root end for intact pieces. Place them on the baking sheet with the delicata squash.

5. Right on the baking sheet, toss the squash and shallots with the 1 tablespoon (15 mL) of olive oil and the minced rosemary, thyme, salt, and pepper. Once the vegetables are evenly coated, slide the baking sheet into the oven. Roast the squash and shallots for approximately 45 minutes, stirring and flipping the vegetables a couple of times, or until all pieces are golden brown and soft. Let the vegetables cool completely.

DRESSING

2 tablespoons (30 mL) balsamic vinegar

salt and pepper, to taste

1 small clove garlic, finely minced or grated with a Microplane grater

1 teaspoon (5 mL) Dijon mustard

2 teaspoons (10 mL) pure maple syrup

¼ cup + 1 tablespoon (50 mL + 15 mL) virgin olive oil

SALAD

1 standard delicata squash

2 to 3 shallots, peeled

1 tablespoon + 2 teaspoons (15 mL + 10 mL) virgin olive oil, divided

1 tablespoon (15 mL) minced fresh rosemary (about 3 sprigs)

2 teaspoons (10 mL) minced fresh thyme leaves (about 4 sprigs)

salt and pepper, to taste

4 cups (1 L) cubed whole-grain sourdough bread (stale bread is preferable)

2 cups (500 mL) sliced lacinato kale

⅓ cup (75 mL) pomegranate seeds

2 stalks celery, thinly sliced

¼ cup (50 mL) leaves from the heart of a celery bunch OR flat-leaf parsley, for garnish

6. While the vegetables are roasting, transfer the bread cubes to the other parchment-lined baking sheet. Toss the bread cubes with the remaining 2 teaspoons (10 mL) of olive oil and the salt and pepper. Once the bread is evenly coated, slide the baking sheet into the oven. Bake the bread pieces, stirring and flipping a couple of times, until evenly golden brown on all sides, about 12 to 14 minutes.

7. In a large serving bowl, combine the cooled roasted squash and shallots, the toasted bread pieces, and the sliced kale, pomegranate seeds, and chopped celery. Drizzle the dressing over top and toss evenly to combine. Let the salad sit for 5 to 10 minutes before serving, so that some of the dressing can permeate the crisp pieces of bread. Roughly chop the celery leaves to garnish the top of the salad. Serve immediately.

Thai-ish Cabbage Salad

SERVES *4 to 6* FREE OF 🌾 🥜

I find that even the pickiest of vegetable eaters are inclined to try a salad with a bunch of thinly shaved vegetables. Throw a bit of sweet fruit into the mix, along with a crunchy component, and you have a crowd pleaser on your hands. This salad does all of those things and if you use a mandoline slicer, it does it in record time. I like making this in the depths of winter when the vegetable selection is starting to feel a bit dull and repetitive. It's like a giant color and flavor bomb for the senses.

1. MAKE THE DRESSING: In a small jar with a tight-fitting lid, combine the lime juice, garlic, ginger, maple syrup, Sriracha, salt, pepper, and grapeseed oil. Tightly secure the lid, and shake the jar vigorously until the dressing has a creamy and smooth consistency. Taste and adjust seasoning, if necessary. Set aside.

2. MAKE THE SALAD: Place the shredded cabbage in a large bowl. Using a vegetable peeler, make long strips from the carrot, and add these to the bowl with the cabbage. Remove the seeds and stem from the bell pepper, cut it into strips, and add these to the bowl.

3. Carefully cut around the large pit of the mango. After you have all of the usable mango you can get, cut the fruit into thin strips and add it to the bowl.

4. Add the sliced green onions. If you like, you can add the mint, cilantro and basil leaves whole to the salad, or you can simply give them a quick chop before adding them. Season the vegetables in the bowl with some salt and pepper, and toss to mix.

5. Pour the dressing over the salad and toss to evenly coat. Garnish the salad with the chopped cashews or peanuts. Serve immediately.

DRESSING

3 tablespoons (45 mL) fresh lime juice

1 clove garlic, finely grated with a Microplane grater

½-inch (1 cm) piece of fresh ginger, peeled and finely grated with a Microplane grater

1 tablespoon (15 mL) pure maple syrup

Sriracha OR other hot sauce, to taste

salt and pepper, to taste

¼ cup + 1 tablespoon (50 mL + 15 mL) grapeseed or other neutral-flavored oil

SALAD

½ head of green or red cabbage, shredded (roughly 5 cups/1.25 L shredded cabbage)

1 large carrot, peeled

1 red bell pepper

1 barely ripe mango, peeled

3 green onions, thinly sliced

¼ cup (50 mL) fresh mint leaves

¼ cup (50 mL) fresh cilantro leaves

¼ cup (50 mL) fresh basil leaves

salt and pepper, to taste

½ cup (125 mL) roasted cashews OR peanuts (or both), chopped, for garnish

Caramelized Onion Potato Salad

SERVES *4 to 6*   FREE OF 🌱 🥜 🌾

Potato salad is a summer picnic staple that can be a touch predict-able, I find. Taking the time to caramelize some onions, bringing their jammy sweetness forward, really takes this version to a higher plane. I make a simple mustard vinaigrette and let the soft onions mingle with it. The pickle addition might seem strange, but I tried a potato salad served this way at a summer barbecue one time and haven't been able to give it up. The naturally sour, dill-imbued flavor makes a lot of sense within the context of potato salad once you try it.

1. MAKE THE DRESSING: In a jar with a tight-fitting lid, combine the olive oil, grainy mustard, horseradish, agave nectar, white wine vinegar, salt, and pepper. Tightly secure the lid, and shake the jar vigorously to combine and set aside.

2. MAKE THE SALAD: Heat the olive oil in a large pot over medium-low heat. Add the onions. Cook the onions, stirring every few minutes, for about 40 minutes or until onions are very soft and deep golden brown. There shouldn't be any dry or crispy bits of onion, and they should appear almost jammy in texture.

3. If the pan is a little dry or the onions are crisping instead of browning, lower the heat slightly and add a splash of water. After the onions are fully caramelized, scrape them into a bowl and allow them to cool.

4. While the onions are caramelizing, place the potatoes in a large saucepan over medium-high heat, and cover them with cold water by 1 inch (2.5 cm). Bring to a boil, uncovered, and then lower the heat to a simmer. Cook the potatoes for 15 minutes or until just tender when pricked with a paring knife.

5. Drain the potatoes and run them under cold water to speed up the cooling process. Once you can handle them, cut the potatoes into quarters, wedges, or bite-sized pieces. Place the cut potatoes in a large bowl.

6. To the potatoes, add the cooled caramelized onions, along with the chopped dill, parsley, green onions, and chopped pickles. Season the salad with salt and pepper.

7. Pour the dressing over the potato salad, and toss to combine. Serve the salad cold or at room temperature.

DRESSING

3 tablespoons (45 mL) virgin olive oil

1 tablespoon (15 mL) grainy mustard

1 teaspoon (5 mL) prepared horseradish

1 teaspoon (5 mL) raw agave nectar OR pure maple syrup

1 tablespoon (15 mL) white wine vinegar

salt and pepper, to taste

SALAD

2 teaspoons (10 mL) virgin olive oil

1 large onion, cut into ¼-inch (5 mm) slices

1½ pounds (681 g) mini new potatoes

¼ cup (50 mL) chopped fresh dill (about 3 sprigs)

¼ cup (50 mL) lightly packed chopped fresh flat-leaf parsley

2 green onions, finely sliced

⅓ cup (75 mL) chopped dill pickles OR bread-and-butter pickles

salt and pepper, to taste

Brussels Sprouts Salad
with Lime and Miso

SERVES *4*   FREE OF 🌿 🥜 🌾

Like most people, I didn't think I enjoyed Brussels sprouts until I tried some with crispy, roasted edges. Now, I grow them in my vegetable garden every year and eat them as often as I can. I make a few versions of this salad, which capitalizes on the interaction of the hot Brussels sprouts and dressing. Miso gives the dressing a well-rounded flavor, and the toasted sunflower seeds add even more crunch and texture. Showered with fresh herbs and creamy avocado, this one makes my fall salad dreams come true. I could eat this whole recipe by myself with ease.

1. Preheat the oven to 400°F (200°C). Line a baking sheet with parchment paper and set aside.

2. MAKE THE DRESSING: In a jar with a tight-fitting lid, combine the lime juice, lime zest, olive oil, Dijon mustard, light miso, maple syrup, salt, and pepper. Tightly secure the lid, and shake the jar vigorously to combine. Mash any remaining lumps of miso with a spoon. Set aside.

3. MAKE THE SALAD: Place the quartered Brussels sprouts onto the baking sheet. Drizzle with the olive oil and season with the chili flakes, salt, and pepper. Toss to coat and slide the baking sheet into the oven. Roast the Brussels sprouts for about 20 to 25 minutes, flipping once at the halfway point. Brussels sprouts should appear evenly charred or browned.

4. Transfer the hot Brussels sprouts to a medium bowl. Pour half of the dressing over the Brussels sprouts, and toss to coat.

5. Transfer the Brussels sprouts to a serving platter. Peel the avocado and remove the pit. Roughly dice the avocado and scatter the pieces on top of the Brussels sprouts. Drizzle the remaining half of the dressing over the salad. Garnish with the chopped mint, chopped basil, toasted sunflower seeds, and minced chili, if using. Serve immediately.

DRESSING

1½ tablespoons (22 mL) fresh lime juice

½ teaspoon (2 mL) lime zest

2 tablespoons (30 mL) virgin olive oil

1 teaspoon (5 mL) Dijon mustard

2 teaspoons (10 mL) mellow or light miso

1 teaspoon (5 mL) pure maple syrup

salt and pepper, to taste

SALAD

1 pound (454 g) Brussels sprouts, trimmed and quartered

2 teaspoons (10 mL) virgin olive oil

½ teaspoon (2 mL) dried chili flakes

salt and pepper, to taste

1 small ripe avocado

GARNISHES

¼ cup (50 mL) chopped fresh mint leaves

¼ cup (50 mL) chopped fresh basil leaves

¼ cup (50 mL) toasted sunflower seeds

minced fresh chili pepper (optional)

Broccoli Caesar
with Smoky Tempeh Bits

SERVES *4* FREE OF 🌾 🥜

On a trip to Montreal with friends, we shared a broccoli-based "Caesar" salad as a starter plate. It featured a whole broccoli stalk that had been charred on a grill, finished in the oven, and then smothered in Caesar dressing. It was so good that I would have fought everyone at the table for the last bite. The smoky tempeh makes this a more filling vegetable course, too.

I blanch the broccoli here, but I've also prepared this salad with roasted broccoli florets as a warm salad. Just place the florets on a baking sheet, toss with a drizzle of olive oil, salt, and pepper, and roast in a 400°F (200°C) oven for about 20 minutes or so.

1. MAKE THE CREAMY CASHEW CAESAR DRESSING: In a jar with a tight-fitting lid, combine the cashew butter, water, lemon juice, salt, and pepper. Stir this mixture with a spoon or small spatula until the cashew butter is broken up. Mash the chunks of cashew butter against the sides of the jar to get it as integrated as possible. Add the garlic, Dijon mustard, capers, nutritional yeast, and olive oil. Tightly secure the lid, and shake the jar vigorously until the dressing has a smooth and creamy consistency. Set aside.

2. MAKE THE SALAD: Bring a large saucepan of water to a boil over medium-high heat. Add a fat pinch of salt and the broccoli florets, and simmer until the broccoli is just tender and bright green, about 4 minutes. Drain the broccoli and run under cold water to stop the cooking process. Set aside.

3. In a small bowl, stir together the paprika, smoked paprika, maple syrup, apple cider vinegar, and tamari. Set aside.

4. Dry the saucepan and return it to the stove over medium heat. Add the oil and let it heat through until it's shimmering slightly. Add the crumbled tempeh, spreading it out to a single layer. Let it sit and brown for a full 2 minutes. Then stir it up, and let it sit another full minute. Pour the paprika mixture into the pan. It should sizzle quite a bit. Stir it to coat all of the tempeh. Remove from the heat.

5. Place the broccoli on your serving platter. Drizzle the Creamy Cashew Caesar Dressing over the top. Scatter the smoky tempeh bits over the top as well. Garnish with some nutritional yeast and freshly ground black pepper to finish. Serve immediately.

CREAMY CASHEW CAESAR DRESSING *(makes extra)*

2 tablespoons (30 mL) raw cashew butter

2 tablespoons (30 mL) filtered water

1½ tablespoons (22 mL) fresh lemon juice

salt and pepper, to taste

3 cloves garlic, grated with a Microplane grater

1 teaspoon (5 mL) Dijon mustard

1 teaspoon (5 mL) minced capers

1 tablespoon (15 mL) nutritional yeast

3 tablespoons (45 mL) virgin olive oil

SALAD

pinch of salt

1 bunch broccoli, cut into florets

1 teaspoon (5 mL) sweet paprika

1 teaspoon (5 mL) smoked paprika

1 teaspoon (5 mL) pure maple syrup

1 teaspoon (5 mL) apple cider vinegar

½ teaspoon (2 mL) gluten-free tamari soy sauce

2 teaspoons (10 mL) virgin olive oil

½ block (4 ounces/114 g) tempeh, crumbled

GARNISHES

2 teaspoons (10 mL) nutritional yeast

freshly ground black pepper

Creamy and Spicy Corn and Millet Toss

SERVES *4 to 5*   FREE OF 🌾🌰

I went to a vegetarian food festival when I first started eating plant-based, and amid all of the meat and cheese imitations that were on offer, there was a small stand selling grilled corn doused in spices, cilantro, and lime. Faux meat has never been my scene personally, so the mere sight of this stand was a huge relief. I ordered two servings and was one happy camper afterward. This salad features some of the same flavors with a bunch of summery extras.

Millet has a slight corn-like flavor, so I love mixing it into fresh corn dishes whenever I can. In this salad, it brings the satiation factor up a bit as well. I prefer to serve a corn sauté or salad at a summer get-together, rather than whole cobs of corn. It helps to stretch the actual corn a bit further and, despite the initial effort, it makes for much less clean-up afterward.

1. In a small saucepan over medium-high heat, combine the millet with 1 cup (250 mL) of filtered water. Bring to a boil. Lower the heat to a simmer, and let the millet cook until all water has been absorbed, about 15 minutes. Let the millet cool.

2. Meanwhile, use a knife to scrape the kernels off the cobs of corn. Heat the olive oil in a cast iron skillet over medium-high heat. Toss the corn into the skillet. Sauté until the corn is just starting to turn golden, about 2 minutes. Season the corn with salt, pepper, and the chili powder. Stir to combine. Add the lime juice and stir once more. Remove from the heat, arrange the corn on a serving platter, and set aside. Wipe out the skillet and return it to the stove over medium-high heat.

3. Place the red bell pepper and poblano pepper into the wiped skillet. Cook the peppers until you get deep-brown char marks on all sides, about 4 to 5 minutes. Place the charred peppers in a small bowl and cover the bowl tightly with plastic wrap. Let the peppers steam for at least 7 to 8 minutes.

4. After the peppers have steamed, remove their stems, seeds, and skins. Cut the peppers into strips and add them to the platter with the corn. Add the cooked and cooled millet to the platter as well.

5. Lightly toss everything on the platter together. Arrange the halved cherry tomatoes on top. Garnish the salad with the chopped cilantro and green onions. Drizzle some of the Creamy Garlic Dressing over the top. Lightly sprinkle the salad with chili powder if you like.

½ cup (125 mL) millet, rinsed

4 cobs of corn

1 teaspoon (5 mL) virgin olive oil

salt and pepper, to taste

1 teaspoon (5 mL) chili powder, plus extra

1 tablespoon (15 mL) fresh lime juice

1 red bell pepper

1 poblano pepper

½ cup (125 mL) cherry tomatoes, halved

Creamy Garlic Dressing (page 98)

GARNISHES

⅓ cup (75 mL) packed roughly chopped fresh cilantro leaves

2 green onions, sliced

chili powder (optional)

Peaches, Peas, and Beans Summer Salad

SERVES *4 to 6*   FREE OF 🌿🥜

Fresh pea season stretches right into summer where I live, so we get to harvest those sweet shell, snow, and snap pea varieties for a while. This is another colorful and vibrant salad that takes advantage of juicy fruit and a crunchy garnish. The dressing is super simple by design, allowing all of the seasonal flavors to shine through.

1. MAKE THE DRESSING: In a small jar with a tight-fitting lid, combine the balsamic vinegar, Dijon mustard, tamari, sunflower oil, salt, and pepper. Tightly secure the lid, and shake the jar vigorously until the dressing has a smooth consistency. Set aside.

2. MAKE THE SALAD: Bring a medium saucepan of water to a boil. Salt the water and then throw in the trimmed green beans. Blanch the beans for 3 minutes or until tender and crisp. Drain the beans and place them in a bowl of ice water to cool immediately.

3. Remove the pits from the peaches and cut the fruit into thin slices. In a large bowl, combine the sliced peaches, shallots, and snap peas. Drain the green beans and lightly dry them. Add the beans to the large bowl. Season the salad with salt and pepper.

4. Pour the dressing over the vegetables and peaches, and toss lightly to combine. Scatter the chopped basil and almonds over the top, and serve.

DRESSING

1 tablespoon (15 mL) balsamic vinegar

1 teaspoon (5 mL) Dijon mustard

1 teaspoon (5 mL) gluten-free tamari soy sauce

2 tablespoons (30 mL) sunflower oil

salt and pepper, to taste

SALAD

¾ pound (341 g) young green (or yellow or burgundy) string beans, trimmed

2 ripe, but firm, peaches

1 small shallot, peeled and sliced paper thin

large handful of snap peas, trimmed and sliced down the middle

salt and pepper, to taste

¼ cup (50 mL) chopped fresh basil leaves

¼ cup (50 mL) whole toasted almonds, coarsely chopped

Go-To Kale Salad *with* "Master Cleanse" Dressing

SERVES *4* FREE OF 🌿 🥜 🌾

The name of this salad is a touch cheeky, only because you can't talk about a cleanse or detox without mentioning kale in the same breath, it seems. The Master Cleanse is a well-known fast that involves drinking a mixture of water, maple syrup, lemon juice, and cayenne pepper for several days. I've never done it, but I *did* try a Master Cleanse-inspired martini at a raw food restaurant one time. It had sake, tons of lemon, a touch of cayenne, and a maple sugar rim. The combination was so delicious! I also enjoyed a citrusy kale salad with shaved fennel that same night, hence the inspiration for this salad.

It might seem unnecessary, but massaging the kale is so important for the outcome of this salad. It helps to soften the leaves and to season them completely before adding the other components.

1. MAKE THE DRESSING: In a small bowl, whisk together the lemon juice, maple syrup, grapeseed oil, cayenne pepper, salt, and pepper, and set aside.

2. MAKE THE SALAD: Place the chopped kale in a large bowl. Pour half of the dressing over top, and season the kale with salt and pepper. Massage the dressing into the kale for about 3 minutes or until the leaves darken and are ever-so-slightly wilted.

3. Add the fennel, apple, and shallot to the bowl, and lightly toss with the kale to distribute.

4. Pour the remaining dressing over the top of the salad, and garnish with the sunflower seeds. Serve immediately.

DRESSING

2 tablespoons (30 mL) fresh lemon juice

1 tablespoon (15 mL) pure maple syrup

3 tablespoons (45 mL) grapeseed or other neutral-flavored oil

¼ teaspoon (1 mL) cayenne pepper

salt and pepper, to taste

SALAD

5 cups (1.25 L) packed chopped kale (from about 1 bunch)

1 small fennel bulb, cored and shaved

1 small sweet apple, cored and shaved

1 small shallot, peeled and shaved

¼ cup (50 mL) sunflower seeds, toasted, for garnish

Shaved Root Salad *with* Crispy Lentils

SERVES 6 FREE OF 🌿 🥜 👣

This is a gorgeous winter salad with some textural interest from cooked lentils that are roasted until crispy and chewy. I turn to root vegetable and cabbage-based salads and slaws in the cold months because I find I'm less likely to crave a leafy, water-heavy salad. It seems that the body naturally craves foods that will help it to seasonally adapt. You can use any mix of root vegetables you like or have on hand.

1. Preheat the oven to 400°F (200°C).

2. MAKE THE DRESSING: In a jar with a tight-fitting lid, combine the olive oil, maple syrup, mustard, water, sherry vinegar, horseradish, garlic, salt, and pepper. Tightly secure the lid, and shake the jar vigorously until the dressing has a creamy and smooth consistency. Set aside.

3. MAKE THE SALAD: Bring a medium saucepan of water to a boil. Drop in the lentils and a big pinch of salt. Bring to a boil again, and then reduce heat to a simmer until lentils are just tender, about 20 minutes. Drain the lentils and spread them out on a kitchen towel to dry.

4. Transfer the dried lentils to a baking sheet. Toss the lentils with the olive oil, salt, and pepper. Slide the baking sheet into the oven, and roast the lentils until they have dried and browned slightly, about 8 minutes. Remove from the oven and set aside.

5. Using a mandoline, slice the beets paper thin and place them in a large bowl. Slice the carrots with the mandoline, and add them to the bowl. Cut the celery root down the middle lengthwise. Slice each half of the celery root with the mandoline, and add the slices to the bowl.

6. Season all the sliced vegetables with salt and pepper, and toss.

7. Toss the sliced vegetables with ⅔ of the dressing. Transfer the dressed vegetables to a serving platter. Scatter the crispy lentils over the vegetables. Pour the remaining dressing over the lentils. Garnish the salad with the fresh dill, and serve immediately.

DRESSING

2 tablespoons (30 mL) virgin olive oil

1 tablespoon (15 mL) pure maple syrup

1 tablespoon (15 mL) grainy mustard

1 tablespoon (15 mL) filtered water

1 tablespoon (15 mL) sherry vinegar OR apple cider vinegar

1 teaspoon prepared horseradish

1 clove garlic, grated with a Microplane grater

salt and pepper, to taste

SALAD

⅓ cup (75 mL) French or black beluga lentils, rinsed

½ teaspoon (2 mL) virgin olive oil

salt and pepper, to taste

2 small beets, peeled (or 1 medium—I use 2 small ones of different colors)

2 medium carrots, peeled

1 small celery root, peeled

2 tablespoons (30 mL) chopped fresh dill (about 2 sprigs), for garnish

Sesame Cucumber Noodles
with Melon and Avocado

SERVES *2*   FREE OF 🌿 🥜 🍚

This is the most refreshing lunch on a hot summer day. The noodles are just julienned slices of cucumber, and they couldn't be simpler to make. I became quite obsessed with an inexpensive julienne peeler one summer and started making every vegetable and fruit I could get my hands on into noodles. This was easily the best experiment from that time. I've swayed even the pickiest of eaters over to the vegetable-loving side with this one. The melon acts like a succulent, almost sweet, dessert-like afterthought to the jumble of savory noodles, which is extra appealing when the heat is on.

1 English cucumber

⅛ teaspoon (0.5 mL) cayenne pepper

salt and pepper, to taste

1 teaspoon (5 mL) fresh lime juice

½ teaspoon (2 mL) hot toasted sesame oil

½ small, ripe cantaloupe, peeled and seeds removed

1 small ripe avocado, peeled and pitted

⅓ cup (75 mL) chopped fresh cilantro leaves, for garnish

1. Using a julienne peeler, make noodle-like strands out of the cucumber. Stop at the seeded center. I typically keep and use this portion of the cucumber for juice or smoothies.

2. Place the cucumber noodles in a medium bowl, and toss them with the cayenne pepper, salt, pepper, lime juice, and hot toasted sesame oil. Let them sit and marinate for 5 minutes.

3. Cut the cantaloupe and avocado into wedges and arrange them on 2 dinner plates. Season the avocado with salt. Divide the cucumber noodles between the plates, draping them over the wedges of melon and avocado.

4. Finish the plates by scattering the chopped cilantro over the top. Serve immediately.

Pepperoncini Lentil Crunch Salad

SERVES *6 to 8*   FREE OF 🌾 🥜 🌰

While snacking on pepperoncini peppers as part of an antipasto plate, I thought to myself, "These would make a delicious salad dressing!" They have spice, acidity, and a touch of sweetness, so they have the perfect balance really. That little hint of heat makes this salad hard to stop eating. I keep the other components of this salad simple and crunchy for extra freshness.

1. MAKE THE DRESSING: Combine the pepperoncini peppers, pepperoncini pickling liquid, white wine vinegar, garlic, ground cumin, maple syrup, olive oil, salt, and pepper in a blender and whiz on high until you have a creamy and smooth mixture. Set aside.

2. MAKE THE SALAD: Fill a medium saucepan with water and bring to a boil. Drop the lentils into the water with a big pinch of salt, and cook until just tender, about 20 minutes. Rinse the lentils with cold water and transfer them to a large bowl.

3. To the bowl, add the bell peppers, onions, celery, and parsley. Season the salad with salt and pepper, and toss to combine.

4. Pour the dressing over the salad, and toss to combine once more. Serve the salad immediately to preserve the crunch of the vegetables, with extra pepperoncini peppers on the side.

DRESSING

4 pepperoncini peppers, stems removed (plus extra for serving)

2 tablespoons (30 mL) pepperoncini pickling liquid

1 tablespoon (15 mL) white wine vinegar

1 clove garlic, chopped

½ teaspoon (2 mL) ground cumin

½ teaspoon (2 mL) pure maple syrup

¼ cup (50 mL) virgin olive oil

salt and pepper, to taste

SALAD

2 cups (500 mL) French or black beluga lentils, rinsed

1 red bell pepper, thinly sliced

1 small red onion, thinly sliced

1 stalk celery, thinly sliced

½ cup (125 mL) roughly chopped fresh flat-leaf parsley

Meyer Lemon Romanesco Glow Salad

SERVES *4 to 6*   FREE OF 🌿 🥣

Meyer lemons have a fragrant and slightly sweeter quality that tastes incredibly clean and fresh with this salad, but you could absolutely use regular lemons. I love the optical and textural illusion of Romanesco broccoli or cauliflower broken up into small bits to emulate couscous or rice. I make this salad when we've been on an indulgent streak or right after the holidays when our taste buds and stomachs need a break.

1. MAKE THE DRESSING: In a small bowl, whisk together the lemon zest, lemon juice, Dijon mustard, grapeseed oil, salt, and pepper until combined. Set aside.

2. MAKE THE SALAD: In batches, use a food processor to blitz the Romanesco florets until you have a couscous-like size and texture. Place the processed Romanesco in a large bowl.

3. To the large bowl, add the apples, celery, grapes, green onions, sage, and walnuts. Season everything with salt and pepper and toss to combine.

4. Pour the dressing over the salad and toss to combine. Serve the salad immediately or store in a container in the refrigerator for up to 3 days.

DRESSING

½ teaspoon (2 mL) Meyer lemon zest

1 tablespoon (15 mL) fresh Meyer lemon juice

½ teaspoon (2 mL) Dijon mustard

2 tablespoons (30 mL) grapeseed or other neutral-flavored oil

salt and pepper, to taste

SALAD

1 medium head Romanesco broccoli (or cauliflower), broken up into florets

1 medium sweet apple, cored and chopped

1 stalk celery, small dice

1 cup (250 mL) seedless grapes, halved

3 green onions, thinly sliced

2 teaspoons (10 mL) minced fresh sage (about 1 sprig)

⅓ cup (75 mL) walnut halves, toasted and chopped

salt and pepper, to taste

Warm Balsamic Mushroom Salad
with Pine Nut Parmesan

SERVES *4*   FREE OF 🌿 🥣

The pine nut parmesan that showers this salad tastes so indulgent. I make it in large batches, sometimes cutting it with raw almonds, to top other salads, pasta, cooked greens, and just about anything else I'm making. The vinaigrette for this salad is made in the pan as you cook the mushrooms, so the warmth of the dressing wilts the arugula just enough when you pour it over. It's a perfect light dinner on a cozy fall night.

1. MAKE THE PINE NUT PARMESAN: Combine the pine nuts, sesame seeds, lemon zest, nutritional yeast, garlic powder, and salt and pepper in a food processor. Whiz on high until you have a crumbly, parmesan-like texture. Set aside.

2. MAKE THE SALAD: Heat 2 tablespoons (30 mL) of the olive oil in a large sauté pan. Throw all of the mushrooms into the pan and let them sit for a full minute. Season the mushrooms with pepper and the minced thyme. Stir and flip the mushrooms and let them sit for another full minute.

3. Add the navy beans to the pan and stir. When the mushrooms begin to glisten and wilt slightly, season with salt and add the garlic to the pan. Stir the mushrooms and beans until garlic is fragrant, about 30 seconds.

4. Add the remaining 3 tablespoons (45 mL) of the olive oil to the pan, along with the balsamic vinegar. Stir everything to combine. The mixture should be moist and lightly juicy.

5. Divide the arugula among 4 dinner plates. Top each mound of arugula with a quarter of the mushrooms and beans, spooning the liquid from the pan over the greens. Finish off each plate with a generous dusting of the Pine Nut Parmesan. Serve warm.

PINE NUT PARMESAN

½ cup (125 mL) raw pine nuts

2 tablespoons (30 mL) sesame seeds

2 teaspoons (10 mL) lemon zest

1 tablespoon (15 mL) nutritional yeast

½ teaspoon (2 mL) garlic powder

salt and pepper, to taste

SALAD

⅓ cup (75 mL) virgin olive oil, divided

1 pound (454 g) cremini mushrooms, stemmed and sliced

salt and pepper, to taste

1 teaspoon (5 mL) minced fresh thyme leaves (about 2 sprigs)

2 cups (500 mL) cooked navy beans

2 cloves garlic, minced

¼ cup (50 mL) balsamic vinegar

4 cups (1 L) packed baby arugula

Hearty Mains & Big Plates

This is the most popular recipe category on my blog by far. Planning a salad, soup, side, or even breakfast is easy when considering plant-based preferences. Mains can be a challenge when coming up with a meal that satisfies but also hits most of the nutritional bases. Even though veganism is more common these days, when people find out that I eat and cook plant-based foods exclusively, I still get questions about adequate protein intake and whether I'm always hungry. Hopefully this section can speak to those questions of satiation because my cooking style seems to favor hearty fare, and these recipes were the most fun to develop (and eat!). There are some casual weeknight bowls with a few easily made components, some company-worthy dishes that require planning, and a few options that lie in the middle.

Vegetables, Chickpeas, and Dumplings

SERVES 5   FREE OF 🥄 🥣

This is the most stick-to-your-ribs kind of recipe that I make. The dumplings on top are light and fluffy despite being made of all whole-grain flour. It's pure winter comfort with celery root forming the bulk of the stew's base. I have made this with chopped new potatoes in place of the celery root with delicious results as well.

1. Heat the olive oil in a heavy-bottomed soup pot over medium heat.

2. MAKE THE STEW: Add the onions, carrots, celery, and leeks. Sauté the vegetables until the onions are translucent and the leeks are quite tender, about 4 minutes. Add the tomato paste, garlic, rosemary, thyme, paprika, and bay leaf, and stir. Cook until the spices are fragrant, about 30 seconds. Add the celery root and chickpeas, and stir. Season the vegetables with salt and pepper.

3. Drizzle the white wine vinegar into the pot, and gently scrape the bottom of the pot to release any accumulated brown bits. Sprinkle the spelt flour over the vegetables. Stir everything until no dry flour spots remain.

4. Add 4 cups (1 L) of the vegetable stock to the pot and stir. Bring to a boil, and then lower the heat to a simmer. Cook the stew, uncovered, for about 20 to 25 minutes or until the cubes of celery root are tender when pierced with a paring knife and the stew itself has thickened up slightly. If the stew seems too thick and pasty, add the remaining 1 cup (250 mL) of vegetable stock.

5. WHILE THE STEW IS SIMMERING, MAKE THE DUMPLING BATTER: In a medium bowl, whisk together the spelt flour, chopped dill, baking powder, sea salt, and pepper. Combine the almond milk, white wine vinegar, and olive oil in a measuring cup, and lightly whisk to combine. Add the almond milk mixture to the bowl, and gently mix with a small spoon until you have a slightly sticky, but still fluid, batter.

6. Make sure your stew is at a gentle simmer before you drop the dumplings in. There shouldn't be any big bubbles coming up. Quickly drop big spoonfuls of the dumpling batter onto the stew, covering the whole surface. You should get 7 or 8 dumplings in total. Put a tight-fitting lid on top, and cook for about 20 to 25 minutes. The dumplings should be firm and springy to the touch when done.

7. Serve the stew hot with the dumplings on top.

STEW

1 tablespoon (15 mL) virgin olive oil

1 medium onion, chopped

2 medium carrots, chopped

1 stalk celery, chopped

2 leeks, light-green and white parts only, chopped

1 tablespoon (15 mL) tomato paste

2 cloves garlic, minced

2 teaspoons (10 mL) minced fresh rosemary (about 2 sprigs)

1 teaspoon (5 mL) dried thyme

1½ teaspoons (7 mL) sweet paprika

1 bay leaf

1 medium celery root, peeled and chopped into ½-inch (1 cm) cubes (about 2 cups/500 mL chopped celery root)

1 cup (250 mL) cooked chickpeas

salt and pepper, to taste

2 teaspoons (10 mL) white wine vinegar

⅓ cup (75 mL) whole spelt flour

4 to 5 cups (1 to 1.25 L) vegetable stock

DUMPLINGS

¾ cup (175 mL) whole spelt flour

1 tablespoon (15 mL) chopped fresh dill (about 1 sprig)

2 teaspoons (10 mL) aluminum-free baking powder

¼ teaspoon (1 mL) fine sea salt

freshly ground black pepper, to taste

½ cup (125 mL) unsweetened almond milk

1 teaspoon (5 mL) white wine vinegar

½ teaspoon (2 mL) virgin olive oil

Creamy Quinoa and White Bean Risotto *with* Crispy Brassica Florets

SERVES *4* FREE OF 🌿 🥜 🥣

I've ordered a few quinoa "risottos" at restaurants, only to be served a heap of sautéed cooked quinoa with some vegetables on top. Where's the creamy, starchy, and cheesy fun in that? What makes traditional risotto so irresistibly good is the creaminess that results from drawing the starch out of Arborio rice through plenty of stirring. Quinoa isn't a naturally starchy grain, so I knew I had to get creative if I was going to make this dish work on my own. I make a simple purée out of cooked white beans with lemon and nutritional yeast, and stir it into the cooked quinoa. Aside from adding protein to a dish that traditionally celebrates carbs, it tastes amazingly creamy.

1. Preheat the oven to 400°F (200°C). Line a baking sheet with parchment paper and set aside.

2. Place the small florets on the baking sheet. Drizzle with 1 tablespoon (15 mL) of the olive oil, and season with salt and pepper. Toss to coat and slide the baking sheet into the oven. Roast the florets until the edges are evenly brown and crispy, flipping the pieces over occasionally to ensure equal doneness, about 20 to 25 minutes. Set aside.

3. While the florets roast, in a blender, purée the white beans with the lemon juice, nutritional yeast, 2 teaspoons (10 mL) of the olive oil, and ⅓ cup (75 mL) of the vegetable stock. As soon as you have a smooth and creamy purée, stop the blender. Set the bean purée aside.

4. Heat the remaining 1 tablespoon (15 mL) of olive oil in a braiser or medium-sized soup pot over medium heat. Add the shallots, and sauté until translucent, about 4 minutes. Add the fresh thyme and stir until fragrant, about 1 minute.

5. Add the rinsed quinoa to the pot and stir to coat in the oil, herbs, and shallots. Then, add the remaining 2 cups (500 mL) of vegetable stock to the pot and stir. Bring to a boil, then simmer until the quinoa has absorbed almost all of the liquid, about 13 to 15 minutes.

(recipe continues)

5 to 6 cups (1.25 to 1.5 L) small (1 to 1½ inch/2.5 to 4 cm) florets of cauliflower OR broccoli OR Romanesco broccoli OR a mix

2 tablespoons + 2 teaspoons (30 mL + 10 mL) virgin olive oil, divided

salt and pepper, to taste

2 cups (500 mL) cooked white beans, such as navy or cannellini

1 tablespoon (15 mL) fresh lemon juice

pinch of nutritional yeast

2⅓ cups (575 mL) vegetable stock, divided

4 to 5 shallots, fine dice (roughly ⅔ cup/150 mL diced shallots)

2 teaspoons (10 mL) minced fresh thyme leaves (about 4 sprigs)

1 cup (250 mL) quinoa (any color), rinsed

½ cup (125 mL) chopped fresh flat-leaf parsley, divided

drizzle of virgin olive oil, for serving (optional)

6. Scrape the white bean purée into the pot and stir to combine. The quinoa should have a creamy consistency without seeming dry. If it seems dry, add a good splash of vegetable stock.

7. Season the risotto with salt and pepper. Add half of the parsley to the pot and stir to mix throughout. Divide the quinoa risotto among 4 bowls. Top all portions of risotto with the crispy roasted florets and remaining parsley. Drizzle a bit of olive oil over the top if you like. Serve hot.

Butternut and Pesto Cream Lasagna

SERVES *6 to 8*   FREE OF 🥣

I love butternut squash and traditional basil pesto together, and seasonally this seems to make sense with my own little garden. I start to get ripe butternut squashes on the sprawling vines when my basil plants are simultaneously growing out of control, right at that abundant collision of summer and fall. This lasagna suits those first cool nights.

1. Preheat the oven to 400°F (200°C). Line a baking sheet with parchment paper and set aside.

2. MAKE THE BUTTERNUT SQUASH SAUCE: Season the squash halves with salt and pepper, and lay them face down on the baking sheet. Bake the squash until tender, about 30 minutes. Remove from the oven and let cool. Lower the oven temperature to 350°F (180°C).

3. Meanwhile, heat the olive oil in a medium sauté pan over medium heat. Add the onions and garlic, and sauté until slightly softened, about 4 minutes. Pour the balsamic vinegar into the pan, and stir to distribute. Remove the pan from the heat, and scrape the mixture into the bowl of a food processor.

4. When it is cool enough to handle, spoon the cooked squash out of the peel and into the food processor with the onion and garlic mixture. Add the vegetable stock to the food processor, and season everything with salt and pepper. Whiz the squash mixture on high until you have a smooth purée. Scrape the squash purée into a bowl and set aside.

5. Rinse the food processor bowl and place it back on the base.

6. MAKE THE PESTO CREAM: In the food processor, combine the white beans, garlic, basil, baby spinach, olive oil, vegetable stock, lemon juice, nutritional yeast, salt, and pepper. Pulse the mixture a few times. Then whiz the cream on high until you have a smooth, green-flecked purée. You may have to stop and scrape the bowl down a couple of times.

7. Cook the lasagna noodles according to package directions. Drain the noodles and cover them in a light slick of olive oil (to avoid sticking). Set aside.

(recipe continues)

BUTTERNUT SQUASH SAUCE

1 butternut squash (2 pounds/1 kg), cut in half lengthwise and seeded

salt and pepper, to taste

1 teaspoon (5 mL) virgin olive oil

1 small onion, chopped

3 cloves garlic, chopped

1 tablespoon (15 mL) balsamic vinegar

⅓ cup (75 mL) vegetable stock

PESTO CREAM

2 cups (500 mL) cooked white beans, such as navy or cannellini

3 cloves garlic, chopped

1 cup (250 mL) packed fresh basil leaves

1 cup (250 mL) packed baby spinach

¼ cup (50 mL) virgin olive oil

¼ cup (50 mL) vegetable stock

2 teaspoons (10 mL) fresh lemon juice

2 teaspoons (10 mL) nutritional yeast

salt and pepper, to taste

ASSEMBLY

9 whole-grain lasagna noodles

1 cup (250 mL) lightly packed baby spinach

⅓ cup (75 mL) pine nuts, toasted (optional—this recipe is nut-free without them)

8. ASSEMBLE THE LASAGNA: In a 13- × 9-inch (3 L) glass or metal dish, lay 3 of the lasagna noodles side by side. Spoon ¼ of the butternut purée over top, and spread it out as evenly as you can. Scatter some baby spinach leaves over the butternut purée. Spoon ⅓ of the pesto cream over the spinach, and spread it out as evenly as possible. Repeat with the remaining noodles, butternut purée, spinach, and pesto cream, ending with the last ¼ of the butternut purée.

9. Cover the lasagna with foil and bake in the oven until heated through, about 50 minutes. Serve squares of lasagna hot with a sprinkle of toasted pine nuts on top.

BBQ Mushroom Toast

SERVES *4* FREE OF 🥜 🌾

Aside from my Tempeh Bacon (page 47) and Eggplant Bacon (page 44), this is about as close as I get to simulating meat in my plant-based kitchen. Mushrooms are popular in plant-based entrées for a reason. Their texture is so rich and satisfying. I eat many versions of mushrooms on toast for dinner when I have to fend for myself, and this recipe is the ultimate. The barbecue sauce couldn't be simpler or faster to make, but it has slow-simmered flavor all the way through.

1. Heat 1 teaspoon (5 mL) of the olive oil in a medium saucepan over medium heat. Grate the onion on the coarse side of a box grater.

2. Scrape the grated onion into the saucepan, trying to get as much of the liquid in the pan as possible. Add the garlic to the pan. Sauté the onions and garlic until the onion shreds appear translucent and soft, about 45 seconds.

3. Add the paprika, mustard powder, and chili powder, and stir. Add the marinara sauce, maple syrup, apple cider vinegar, and tamari to the saucepan. Stir to combine. Bring to a boil, and then reduce the heat and simmer until the sauce has slightly thickened, about 3 minutes. Keep the sauce warm.

3. Heat the remaining 2 teaspoons (10 mL) of olive oil in a large sauté pan over medium heat. Remove the stems from the mushrooms, and slice the caps into thin strips. Add the sliced mushrooms to the pan, and season them with pepper.

4. Let the mushrooms sit for about 1 minute before stirring them. The oil should be fully absorbed. Stir the mushrooms frequently. Once the volume of the mushrooms has reduced by half and the slices are glistening, season them with salt. Sauté for another minute or until the mushrooms are completely soft.

5. Scrape the BBQ sauce into the saucepan with the mushrooms, and stir to combine. Keep the saucy mushroom mixture warm while you toast the 4 slices of bread.

6. Set a slice of toast on a plate, and spoon a quarter of the saucy mushrooms on top. Repeat with the remaining toast and mushrooms. Serve hot.

---

3 teaspoons (15 mL) virgin olive oil, divided

1 small onion, peeled

1 clove garlic, minced

½ teaspoon (2 mL) sweet paprika

½ teaspoon (2 mL) mustard powder

1 teaspoon (5 mL) chili powder

1½ cups (375 mL) jarred marinara sauce OR crushed tomatoes

¼ cup (50 mL) pure maple syrup

2 tablespoons (30 mL) apple cider vinegar

1 teaspoon (5 mL) gluten-free tamari soy sauce

1½ pounds (681 g) mixed mushrooms (I like a mix of shiitake and cremini)

salt and pepper, to taste

4 thick slices whole-grain bread (gluten-free if required)

Spicy Curry Tempeh Patties

SERVES 6 FREE OF 🌿 💧 🌾

This recipe makes a flavorful veggie burger that holds together perfectly, but I mostly just love to enjoy these patties over a big bed of greens with a hearty drizzle of my Creamy Garlic Dressing (page 98) and some hot sauce. I usually advise on steaming tempeh before you cook it, because it opens up the protein's "pores" so that it can absorb more flavor. In this case, the tempeh is blitzed up with chilies, spices, ginger, and cilantro for some real oomph, so the pre-steaming is unnecessary.

1. Preheat the oven to 350°F (180°C).

2. In a food processor, combine the shallots, garlic, chili peppers, ginger, green onions, cilantro, and curry powder. Blitz this mixture on high until you have a rough paste. Add the tempeh, lime juice, agave nectar, and tomato paste. Blitz the machine on high again until all of the tempeh is chopped finely and well integrated into the spice paste. Sprinkle the chickpea flour into the food processor, and season the mixture with salt and pepper. Pulse the food processor until you have a sticky paste with no dry flour in the mix.

3. Lightly flour your hands with some extra chickpea flour, and form the mixture into 6 patties. Place the patties onto a baking sheet and place in the oven. Bake the patties for 30 to 35 minutes, or until they appear slightly dried around the edges and firm. Flip the patties over halfway through baking.

4. Serve the patties hot on whole-grain buns or beds of greens with the Creamy Garlic Dressing and other accompaniments of your choice.

1 block (8 ounces/227 g) tempeh, cut into 1-inch (2.5 cm) cubes

3 shallots, chopped (about ½ cup/125 mL)

3 cloves garlic, chopped

2 small red chili peppers, seeded and chopped

1-inch (2.5 cm) piece of fresh ginger, peeled and chopped

3 green onions, chopped

¼ cup (50 mL) lightly packed fresh cilantro leaves

2 teaspoons (10 mL) curry powder

1 tablespoon (15 mL) fresh lime juice

1 teaspoon (5 mL) raw agave nectar

1 tablespoon (15 mL) tomato paste

3 tablespoons (45 mL) chickpea flour

salt and pepper, to taste

whole-grain buns or beds of greens, for serving (gluten-free if required)

Creamy Garlic Dressing (page 98)

Rice and Bean Veggie Burgers

SERVES *8*   FREE OF 🌿🫛💧🍚   REQUIRES *time for prep*

This is our go-to veggie burger. I always know that it will hold together, and the parcooked rice makes for crispy edges. I prefer baking these patties for less fuss. I find sautéing them means using quite a bit of oil between batches. These burgers will fall through the grates if cooked directly on a grill. If I'm cooking a bunch of things on the grill already and I'm in the mood, I place a big, doubled sheet of aluminum foil directly onto the grates, spray it with canola oil, and "bake" the burgers on that for about 25 minutes, carefully flipping them over halfway through.

1. Place the rice in a medium saucepan, and cover it with 2 cups (500 mL) of filtered water. Bring to a boil over medium heat. Lower the heat to a simmer and cook the rice for 15 minutes. It should still be quite chewy but not hard. Drain the rice if necessary, and scrape into a large bowl. Set aside.

2. In a food processor, combine the sunflower seeds, garlic, red onions, grated carrots, and beans. Pulse the machine until you have a chunky paste. Add this paste into the large bowl with the rice.

3. To the rice and paste mixture, add the nutritional yeast, oat flour, arrowroot powder, spices, herbs, tomato paste, tamari, 1 tablespoon (15 mL) of the filtered water, salt, and pepper. Mix everything with your hands until the mixture holds together when you pinch it. Add more filtered water if necessary.

4. Form the mixture into 8 equal patties. Refrigerate the patties for at least 1 hour so that they can properly set.

5. Preheat the oven to 350°F (180°C).

6. Remove the patties from the refrigerator, and place them on a baking sheet. Bake the veggie burgers for 30 minutes, flipping them at the halfway point. They should be evenly browned, lightly crispy at the edges, and firm. Serve veggie burgers hot with accompaniments.

1 cup (250 mL) uncooked medium-grain brown rice

½ cup (125 mL) raw sunflower seeds

5 cloves garlic, peeled

¾ cup (175 mL) chopped red onion

½ cup (125 mL) grated carrots

¾ cup (175 mL) cooked and drained beans of choice

2 tablespoons (30 mL) nutritional yeast

2 tablespoons (30 mL) certified gluten-free oat flour

2 teaspoons (10 mL) arrowroot powder

4 teaspoons ground spices of choice, such as cumin, coriander, za'atar, and Old Bay seasoning

¼ cup (50 mL) chopped fresh leafy herbs of your choice, such as basil, cilantro, and parsley

2 tablespoons (30 mL) tomato paste

4 teaspoons (20 mL) gluten-free tamari soy sauce

1 to 2 tablespoons (15 to 30 mL) filtered water

salt and pepper, to taste

Squash Parcels *with* Almond Quinoa

SERVES *4* FREE OF 🌿 🍚

This elegant main employs a simple but fancy-appearing technique called *en papillote*. It's a cute individual paper package filled with whatever vegetable or protein you're cooking, aromatics, spices, and citrus or some other acidic component. Carefully cutting the packages open at the table lets the fragrant steam escape. It's an experience! Once you have the folding technique down, you can try all sorts of combinations.

1. Preheat the oven to 400°F (200°C).

2. CUT THE PARCHMENT PAPER: Take one sheet of parchment, fold it in half, and cut out the shape of half a heart so that when you unfold the paper, the cut-out is heart-shaped. Repeat with the remaining parchment pieces.

3. MAKE THE SQUASH MIXTURE: Peel the butternut squash. Cut it in half lengthwise and scoop out the seeds. Cut the squash into 1-inch (2.5 cm) cubes. Place the squash in a large bowl, and add the garlic, olive oil, smoked paprika, thyme, chili flakes, salt, and pepper. Toss to combine.

4. Take one piece of pre-cut parchment paper, and place one side of the heart shape on a large baking sheet. Spoon a quarter of the squash mixture onto the center of the paper toward the crease. Place 1 lemon slice and 3 olives on top of the squash. Fold the other side of the heart over the ingredients. Working from the top of the heart, begin tightly folding the open edge of the paper. Continue folding around the open edge of the paper to form a seal. Repeat this process with the remaining parchment, squash mixture, lemon slices, and olives.

5. Slide the baking sheet of packages into the oven. Bake the parcels for 30 minutes.

6. MAKE THE ALMOND QUINOA: Place the quinoa in a medium saucepan over medium-high heat. Cover the quinoa with the filtered water. Bring to a boil and then reduce the heat to a simmer until the quinoa has absorbed all the water, about 15 minutes.

FOR ASSEMBLY

4 pieces of parchment paper about the size of a half-pint pan

SQUASH

1 medium (1½ pounds/681 g) butternut squash

1 clove garlic, thinly sliced

1 tablespoon (15 mL) virgin olive oil

1 teaspoon (5 mL) smoked paprika

1 teaspoon (5 mL) fresh thyme leaves (about 2 sprigs)

¼ teaspoon (1 mL) dried chili flakes

salt and pepper, to taste

4 lemon slices

12 green olives

ALMOND QUINOA

¾ cup (175 mL) quinoa, rinsed

1½ cups (375 mL) filtered water

1 teaspoon (5 mL) virgin olive oil

1 teaspoon (5 mL) fresh lemon juice

⅓ cup (75 mL) packed fresh flat-leaf parsley

⅓ cup (75 mL) packed arugula

salt and pepper, to taste

¼ cup (50 mL) almonds, toasted and chopped

7. Remove the quinoa from the heat, and toss it with the olive oil and lemon juice. Roughly chop the parsley and arugula, and stir them into the quinoa. Season with salt and pepper.

8. ASSEMBLE THE SQUASH PARCELS AND QUINOA: Place one squash parcel on each plate. Carefully snip the top of the parcel with scissors and pull the paper back, being careful to avoid the steam. Serve ¼ of the herbed quinoa on the side. Sprinkle ¼ of the almonds over each portion of squash quinoa.

Crispy Avocado Tacos

SERVES *4 to 5*   FREE OF 🌿 🥥

I love a vegan taco with a clever and saucy mushroom/bean/lentil/tofu/tempeh filling. If the taco has an avocado-based topping though—either simply sliced, made into a crema, or some kind of guacamole, that's always my favorite part. For this main, I coat the wedges of ripe avocado in crushed-up, seasoned rice crackers for a very satisfying crunch. The finish of my Creamy Garlic Dressing (page 98) is the perfect complement.

1. Place the rice crackers in the bowl of a food processor. Blitz the crackers on high until they take on the texture of breadcrumbs. Pour the cracker crumbs out into a pie dish or other plate with a lip. Mix the chili powder, cumin, garlic powder, salt, and pepper into the cracker crumbs.

2. Cut the avocados in half lengthwise and extract the pits. Cut the halves into quarters. Then, cut those quarters in half as well. You should have 16 wedges total. Carefully remove the peel from each avocado wedge.

3. Place the avocado wedges in the dish with the cracker crumbs, and carefully turn them over to coat with crumbs on all sides. Lightly press the crumbs into the avocado to make them stick. Once you have all wedges coated, transfer them to a clean plate.

4. For each taco, take one warm corn tortilla and lay an avocado wedge down the middle. Pack a small amount of cabbage next to the avocado wedge. Scatter some red onion slices, cilantro leaves, and radish slices on top. Finish the taco with a drizzle of Creamy Garlic Dressing, some dabs of hot sauce if you like, and lime wedges. Enjoy immediately.

2 cups (500 mL) rice crackers

½ teaspoon (2 mL) chili powder

½ teaspoon (2 mL) ground cumin

½ teaspoon (2 mL) garlic powder

salt and pepper, to taste

2 large ripe, but firm, avocados

16 small (6-inch/15 cm) corn tortillas, warmed

2 cups (500 mL) shredded cabbage

½ small red onion, thinly sliced

½ cup (125 mL) fresh cilantro leaves

2 to 4 radishes, thinly sliced

1 batch Creamy Garlic Dressing (page 98) made with fresh lime juice instead of lemon

hot sauce, for serving (optional)

lime wedges, for serving

Roasted Chili Basil Lime Tofu Bowls

SERVES *4* FREE OF 🌿 🥜 🍚

Most nights, dinner is an amalgamation of several parts nestled into a big bowl at my house. I usually have a cooked grain and some kind of plant protein on hand. From there, I mix those elements with a sauce or dressing, seasonal vegetables, and some kind of topping (such as chopped nuts, seeds, or sprouts). This bowl uses my favorite cooking method for tofu: roasting. It's so easy and takes care of those craveable crispy edges without using excessive oil. With the bold flavors here, this makes our typical weeknight bowl meal feel special.

1. Preheat the oven to 400°F (200°C). Line a baking sheet with parchment paper and set aside.

2. Drain the tofu of its packing liquid and pat dry with a kitchen towel. Cut tofu into 1-inch (2.5 cm) cubes.

3. In a medium bowl, whisk the lime zest, lime juice, grapeseed oil, garlic powder, chili flakes, salt, and pepper together until combined.

4. Toss the tofu in the lime and oil mixture to coat. Remove the tofu cubes from the bowl with your hands, reserving as much of the lime and oil mixture as possible. Transfer the tofu cubes to the baking sheet. Spread them out and slide the baking sheet into the oven.

5. Roast the tofu for 15 minutes. Remove the baking sheet from the oven, and gently flip the tofu cubes over. Toss the broccoli florets in the lime and oil mixture, and transfer them to the baking sheet as well. Slide the baking sheet back into the oven. Roast the tofu and broccoli until all edges are lightly browned, another 20 minutes.

6. Whisk the basil into the remaining lime and oil mixture.

7. Serve the roasted tofu and broccoli hot over bowls of brown rice with sprouts, toasted sunflower seeds, and drizzles of the basil-flecked lime and oil mixture.

1 block (14 ounces/398 g) extra-firm tofu

2 teaspoons (10 mL) lime zest

2 tablespoons (30 mL) fresh lime juice

2 tablespoons (30 mL) grapeseed or other neutral-flavored oil

½ teaspoon (2 mL) garlic powder

½ teaspoon (2 mL) chili flakes

salt and pepper, to taste

2 cups (500 mL) broccoli florets

¼ cup (50 mL) chopped fresh basil leaves

2 cups (500 mL) cooked brown rice

½ cup (125 mL) fresh sprouts (I use sunflower sprouts)

¼ cup (50 mL) toasted sunflower seeds

Eggplant "Bolognese" Pasta

SERVES *4* FREE OF 🥜 🍚

I came up with this recipe when I had too many eggplants in my garden at the end of one really hot summer, just when the nights were starting to get cool enough to enjoy a pasta dish with substance. I love that this one is weeknight-simple, but lovely enough for guests, without question. Sometimes I toss a cup or so of cooked lentils into the sauce at the end for a hit of protein. I salt and rinse the eggplant to get rid of any bitterness, and to greatly improve the texture as well. The addition of some chopped olives really brings out the meaty nature of eggplant. I don't particularly aim for meat-like results when I cook, but this dish goes in that direction in a very organic way.

1 large eggplant, diced into ½-inch (1 cm) cubes

sea salt

¼ cup + 1 tablespoon (50 mL + 15 mL) virgin olive oil, divided

salt and pepper, to taste

5 cloves garlic, minced

½ teaspoon (2 mL) chili flakes

¼ teaspoon (1 mL) dried oregano

1 can (28 ounces/796 mL) crushed tomatoes

1 cup (250 mL) vegetable stock OR water

¾ pound (341 g) whole-grain or gluten-free long pasta of your choice, such as spaghetti or linguini

6 whole fresh basil leaves, plus extra chopped, for garnish

½ cup (125 mL) pitted Kalamata olives, finely chopped

1. Preheat the oven to 400°F (200°C). Line a baking sheet with parchment paper and set aside.

2. In a large bowl, toss the diced eggplant with a generous sprinkle of sea salt. Let the eggplant sit for 10 minutes to release some of its water. Pour the salted eggplant into a colander and rinse with fresh water. Dry the eggplant pieces as thoroughly as you can with a kitchen towel, and then lay them on the prepared baking sheet.

3. Toss the eggplant with 1 tablespoon (15 mL) of the olive oil and the salt and pepper. Spread the eggplant out into a single layer. Slide the baking sheet into the oven, and roast until the eggplant is tender and has browned slightly, about 20 minutes. Set aside.

4. In a large, deep skillet (or braiser), heat the remaining ¼ cup (50 mL) of olive oil over medium heat. Add the garlic, stir, and sauté for about 30 seconds or until fragrant. Add the chili flakes and oregano, and stir. Add the tomatoes and vegetable stock to the skillet, and stir to combine. Bring to a boil, uncovered. Lower the heat and simmer the sauce for 30 minutes.

5. Meanwhile, cook the pasta according to package directions. Drain and set aside.

(recipe continues)

6. Drop the basil leaves into the tomato sauce and submerge the leaves. Cover the sauce and let it continue to cook for 10 more minutes.

7. Remove the basil leaves from the sauce, and season it with salt and pepper. Add the roasted eggplant and chopped olives to the sauce, and stir to distribute. Carefully toss the cooked pasta in the sauce. After the noodles are coated in sauce, sprinkle the chopped basil on top. Serve the pasta hot.

Pot-Roasted Celery Root *with* Horseradish Cream

SERVES *4*   FREE OF 🌿 🥣

Celery root, or celeriac, is my favorite vegetable. It has the creamy, starchy quality of a potato but so much more flavor. Plus, it has a diamond-in-the-rough vibe because of its gnarly appearance. I grow the roots in my garden and look forward to pulling them up every fall. This pot-roasting method is perfect for a special cool weather dinner, as it does take a little bit of extra time. You start the dish on the stove, transfer it to the oven, and then move back to the stove to make a reduction of apple cider. The steps are easy enough and worth it for the tender slices of celery root nestled into sticky cider and onions, all drizzled with creamy horseradish sauce and showered with hazelnuts.

1. Preheat the oven to 350°F (180°C).

2. MAKE THE POT-ROASTED CELERY ROOT: Heat the olive oil over medium heat in a large, heavy-bottomed, ovenproof pot. Drop the onions, leeks, thyme, and apples into the pot. Stir and sauté the mixture until the onions are soft and translucent, about 6 to 7 minutes.

3. Peel the rough exterior off of the celery roots. If using small celery roots, nestle them into the pot whole among the vegetables and apples. If you have 2 large celery roots, cut them in half lengthwise before nestling them into the pot.

4. Season liberally with salt and pepper. Pour 2 cups (500 mL) of the apple cider into the pot, along with the tamari and apple cider vinegar. The liquid should go halfway up the celery roots. Add more apple cider if necessary.

5. Put a tight-fitting lid on the pot, and carefully transfer the pot to the oven. Roast the celery roots for 1 hour, removing the pot at the halfway point to rotate the celery roots and lightly stir the vegetables. The celery roots should be tender enough to pierce with a knife right through to the center.

(recipe continues)

POT-ROASTED CELERY ROOT

1 tablespoon (15 mL) virgin olive oil

1 medium yellow onion, sliced

2 leeks, white and light-green parts only, sliced

2 teaspoons (10 mL) fresh thyme leaves (about 4 sprigs)

1 small apple, cored and thinly sliced

4 small celery roots, peeled (or 2 large—about 3½ pounds/1.75 kg celery root total)

salt and pepper, to taste

2 to 3 cups (500 to 750 mL) apple cider

1 teaspoon (5 mL) gluten-free tamari soy sauce

1 teaspoon (5 mL) apple cider vinegar

HORSERADISH CREAM

¼ cup (50 mL) raw cashew butter

¼ cup (50 mL) filtered water

2 tablespoons (30 mL) prepared horseradish

2 teaspoons (10 mL) Dijon mustard

salt and pepper, to taste

FOR SERVING

¼ cup (50 mL) chopped fresh flat-leaf parsley

¼ cup (50 mL) toasted hazelnuts, chopped

6. Retrieve the celery roots from the pot and transfer them to a cutting board. Place the pot on the stove over medium heat. There should still be quite a bit of liquid in the pot (along with the vegetables and apples). Bring to a boil, uncovered, and then simmer until liquid is reduced by ⅔, about 22 to 25 minutes.

7. Cut the celery roots into 1-inch (2.5 cm) slices. Nestle the slices in the reduced apple cider and vegetables. Season the exposed slices with salt and pepper.

8. MAKE THE HORSERADISH CREAM: In a medium bowl, whisk together the cashew butter, filtered water, horseradish, Dijon mustard, salt, and pepper. Mix ingredients until you have a smooth, creamy texture.

9. Serve slices of the pot-roasted celery root with portions of the apple cider reduction and vegetables, topped with the horseradish cream, chopped parsley, and hazelnuts.

Creamy Harissa Lentils *with* Cauliflower Rice

SERVES *4 to 5*   FREE OF 🌿 🥜 🍚

There was a dish at the farm-to-table restaurant I worked at that used a spicy, deep red harissa. Just the sheer mention of it gives me an aroma memory of carrying the dish to the waiting table with the chili and caraway smells wafting toward me. I make the spicy sauce at home all the time now and find that it tastes incredible with a variety of plant proteins and vegetables that veer toward sweet when cooked.

One of the most popular recipes on my site is a raw cauliflower "rice" dish. Since I posted that one, I've realized that I prefer riced cauliflower to be lightly cooked. It takes away some of that cabbage-like aroma and improves the texture as well. I detail my method for making it this way here.

1. MAKE THE HARISSA: In a dry skillet over medium heat, stir and toast the caraway, cumin, and coriander seeds until fragrant and nutty-smelling, about 2 minutes. Transfer the toasted spices to a food processor. Add the chili peppers, tomato paste, lemon zest, lemon juice, garlic, olive oil, salt, and pepper, and whiz on high until you have a smooth paste. Scrape the harissa into a bowl and set aside. Rinse the food processor bowl.

2. Fill a medium saucepan with water and bring to a boil. Add the lentils and a good pinch of salt. Simmer the lentils until they are just tender, about 20 minutes. Drain and return the lentils to the saucepan.

3. To the lentils, add ¾ cup (175 mL) of the harissa. Stir the mixture, and bring to a strong simmer. Keep the mixture warm, and add more harissa if necessary to achieve a creamy, saucy texture.

4. MAKE THE CAULIFLOWER RICE: Place the chopped cauliflower in the food processor, and pulse until you have a uniform, rice-like texture throughout.

5. Heat the olive oil in a large sauté pan over medium heat. Add the riced cauliflower, and season with salt and pepper. Add a splash of water to the pan to create some steam. Stir the cauliflower until it has softened around the edges just a bit, about 1 minute. Remove from the heat and toss it with the parsley, mint, green onions, and lemon juice.

6. Divide the cauliflower rice among 4 plates. Top each portion with ¼ of the harissa lentils. Serve warm.

HARISSA (*makes extra*)

3 tablespoons (45 mL) caraway seeds

3 tablespoons (45 mL) cumin seeds

3 tablespoons (45 mL) coriander seeds

3 to 4 small red chili peppers, seeded and chopped

2 tablespoons (30 mL) tomato paste

1 tablespoon (15 mL) lemon zest

⅓ cup (75 mL) fresh lemon juice

2 cloves garlic, chopped

⅓ cup (75 mL) virgin olive oil

salt and pepper, to taste

1 cup (250 mL) French or black beluga lentils, rinsed

CAULIFLOWER RICE

5 cups (1.25 L) chopped cauliflower florets (from 1 small head)

1 teaspoon (5 mL) virgin olive oil

salt and pepper, to taste

¼ cup (50 mL) chopped fresh flat-leaf parsley

¼ cup (50 mL) chopped fresh mint leaves

2 green onions, thinly sliced

2 teaspoons (10 mL) fresh lemon juice

Tandoori-Rubbed Portobellos
with Cool Cilantro Sauce

SERVES *4* FREE OF 🌿 🥜 🍚 REQUIRES *time to soak*

This main looks deceptively meaty on the plate, and it satisfies on the same level. I buy a tandoori spice mixture from a local company, and the intense spicy flavor of it meets its match with rich, unctuous portobello mushrooms cooked on the grill. The cool cilantro sauce offers a creamy counterpoint and is entirely sunflower-seed based. Cashews tend to be the go-to for creamy vegan sauces, but I find sunflower seeds to be just as effective, and as a bonus, they're typically more affordable.

If you don't have access to a grill, you can certainly roast the marinated mushrooms in a 400°F (200°C) oven for 20 minutes, and then finish them under the broiler for 1 minute per side for a similar effect.

1. **MAKE THE COOL CILANTRO SAUCE:** Drain the sunflower seeds and transfer them to a blender. Add the filtered water, garlic, lime juice, and olive oil. Whiz the mixture on high until you have a mostly smooth purée. Stop to scrape down the sides or add another tablespoon of water if necessary. Scrape the sauce base out of the blender into a small bowl. Stir in the cilantro, green onions, salt, and pepper. Cover and place in the refrigerator until you're ready to use it.

2. Preheat a grill to high.

3. **PREPARE THE PORTOBELLOS:** Take the portobello mushroom caps and, using a spoon, scrape out the gills—the dark brown strips that line the underside of the mushroom. Transfer the scraped mushrooms to a plate.

4. In a medium bowl, whisk together the olive oil, lime juice, tandoori spice, ginger, garlic, salt, and pepper. Rub this wet spice mixture on both sides of the portobello mushrooms.

5. Lightly rub some oil on the grill with a wad of paper towel. Place the spice-rubbed portobello caps on the grill and close the lid. Let the portobellos cook for 4 minutes, then flip them over. Cook for another 4 minutes. The mushrooms should be tender, be lightly glistening, and have char marks on both sides. Remove from the grill.

6. Slice the grilled portobellos, and serve with Cool Cilantro Sauce, warm rice, and extra chopped cilantro.

COOL CILANTRO SAUCE

½ cup (125 mL) raw sunflower seeds, soaked for at least 4 hours

¼ cup + 2 tablespoons (50 mL + 30 mL) filtered water

1 clove garlic, finely grated with a Microplane grater

1 tablespoon (15 mL) fresh lime juice

1 tablespoon (15 mL) virgin olive oil

¼ cup (50 mL) finely chopped fresh cilantro leaves

1 green onion, white and light-green parts only, thinly sliced

salt and pepper, to taste

PORTOBELLOS

4 large portobello mushroom caps

2 tablespoons (30 mL) virgin olive oil

1 tablespoon (15 mL) fresh lime juice

1 tablespoon (15 mL) tandoori spice blend

1-inch (2.5 cm) piece of fresh ginger, peeled and finely grated with a Microplane grater

1 clove garlic, finely grated with a Microplane grater

salt and pepper, to taste

FOR SERVING

warm cooked brown rice

chopped fresh cilantro leaves

Vegetable and Bean Pot Pies
with Potato Crusts

SERVES 5 FREE OF 🥜 🍚

I find vegan pastry particularly hard to master without the use of vegetable shortening, vegan margarine, and the like. I stay away from these ingredients, and an oil-based crust can be a tricky, messy beast. I skip the whole thing here and just slice sweet and regular potatoes into thin coins, fan them out on top of this vegetable and bean pot pie, and roast them until crispy and crust-like. The result has all of the effect of a traditional pot pie with much less effort.

1 tablespoon (15 mL) virgin olive oil, divided

1 medium yellow onion, small dice

1 medium carrot, small dice

1 stalk celery, small dice

4 cloves garlic, minced

1 teaspoon (5 mL) minced fresh rosemary (about 1 sprig)

1 teaspoon (5 mL) tomato paste

1 medium zucchini, cut into ½-inch (1 cm) cubes

1½ cups (375 mL) cooked white beans, such as navy, cannellini, or butter beans

2 tablespoons (30 mL) dry white wine

salt and pepper, to taste

3 tablespoons (45 mL) whole spelt flour

1½ cups (375 mL) vegetable stock

1 medium sweet potato OR 6 to 7 mini new potatoes, thinly sliced, or a mixture

1. Preheat the oven to 375°F (190°C). Place 5 ramekins or ovenproof dishes with 1 cup (250 mL) capacity on a baking sheet and set aside.

2. Heat half of the olive oil in a large pot over medium heat. Add the onions, carrots, and celery, and sauté until the onions are slightly softened, about 3 minutes. Add the garlic, rosemary, and tomato paste, and stir. Add the zucchini and white beans to the pot. Stir to combine. Pour in the white wine, and scrape up any browned bits from the bottom of the pot. Season the stew with salt and pepper.

3. Sprinkle the spelt flour over the vegetables and beans. Stir until the flour is moistened and is starting to get slightly pasty. Pour in the vegetable stock. Bring to a boil and then reduce to a simmer until slightly thickened, stirring occasionally, about 4 minutes.

4. Divide the stew among the ramekins. Arrange sweet potato slices on top of the ramekins in a fan or layered pattern. This will form your top crust. Gently brush the sweet potato slices with the remaining oil. Season the crusts with salt and pepper.

5. Slide the pot pies into the oven, and bake until the filling is bubbling and the sweet potato slices are tender and lightly browned on the edges, about 30 to 35 minutes.

6. Serve the pot pies hot.

Farro and Pine Nut Chard Rolls

SERVES *4* FREE OF 🥣

Chard grows like a weed in my garden, and aside from juicing the leaves and sautéing them with garlic, I don't do much with it. The big beautiful leaves make a flexible wrap for any kind of filling once you blanch them a bit. This dish puts the chard into a main course with chewy farro and toasted pine nuts all stuffed inside.

1 cup (250 mL) semi-pearled farro

¼ cup (50 mL) pine nuts, toasted and chopped

1 teaspoon (5 mL) lemon zest

1 teaspoon (5 mL) nutritional yeast

1 tablespoon (15 mL) virgin olive oil

1 tablespoon (15 mL) fresh lemon juice

salt and pepper, to taste

8 chard leaves

2 cups (500 mL) prepared marinara sauce (you could make the sauce from the Eggplant "Bolognese" Pasta recipe, page 151, right up to the point before the eggplant is added)

1. Preheat the oven to 350°F (180°C). Set out an ovenproof 11- × 7-inch (2 L) ceramic or metal baking dish.

2. Place the farro in a medium saucepan. Cover with water by about 1 inch (2.5 cm). Bring to a boil and then reduce the heat and simmer, uncovered, until the farro is just tender, about 28 minutes. Drain any excess water from the farro and return it to the saucepan, off the heat.

3. Using the saucepan as a mixing bowl, stir in the pine nuts, lemon zest, nutritional yeast, olive oil, lemon juice, salt, and pepper. Set aside.

4. Take one chard leaf and remove the stem. You should have two long halves of the leaf now. Repeat with remaining chard leaves. Place all trimmed chard in a large bowl. Cover the chard with boiling water and let it sit to wilt for 5 minutes. Drain the water and pat the chard dry.

5. Spread ½ cup (125 mL) of marinara sauce on the bottom of the baking dish.

6. Take one trimmed chard segment and spoon 2 to 3 tablespoons (30 to 45 mL) of the farro mixture onto the bottom of the leaf. Tuck the leaf over the filling and tightly roll up. Place the chard roll into the baking dish, seam side down, on top of the sauce. Repeat this process with the remaining farro filling and chard.

7. Once you've filled the baking dish, spread the remaining marinara on top of the chard rolls. Carefully pour ½ cup (125 mL) of water over the chard rolls as well. Cover the baking dish with foil and place in the oven.

8. Bake the chard rolls for 30 minutes or until the chard is wilted and the sauce is bubbling at the edges.

9. Serve the chard rolls hot.

Spice-Crusted Cauliflower
with Walnut Sauce

SERVES *2*   FREE OF 🌿 🍚

I remember when cauliflower "steak" recipes took over the internet a couple of years ago. They look so beautiful sliced down the middle—almost like trees. And like any vegetable from the brassica family, cauliflower tastes incredible with some char on the edges, so the "steak" frenzy made so much sense. I serve these with a simple, lightly rich, toasted walnut sauce. All the ingredients just go in the blender, and a pillowy swoop of sauce looks so impressive beneath the spiced and charred cauliflower.

1. Preheat the oven to 350°F (180°C).

2. MAKE THE WALNUT SAUCE: In a large, ovenproof skillet, toast the walnuts over medium heat until fragrant and slightly darkened, about 5 minutes. Transfer the walnuts to a blender. Return the skillet to the stove. Heat 1 teaspoon (5 mL) of the olive oil. Add the onions and garlic. Sauté until the edges of the onion are just starting to soften, about 2 minutes. Scrape the onions and garlic into the blender.

3. Add the almond milk, lemon juice, salt, and pepper to the blender, and whiz the mixture on high until you have a smooth and creamy sauce. Keep the sauce warm while you prepare the cauliflower.

4. MAKE THE SPICE-CRUSTED CAULIFLOWER: Cut two 1-inch-thick (2.5 cm) "steaks" from the center of the cauliflower. You should have a nice cross-section of the vegetable that holds together. Moisten the steaks lightly with water and season with paprika, thyme, salt, and pepper on both sides.

5. Heat the remaining olive oil in the skillet over medium-high heat. Carefully add the cauliflower steaks, and sear until evenly browned on one side, about 3 minutes. Flip the cauliflower over and transfer the skillet to the oven.

6. Cook the cauliflower in the oven until the center core or stem section is tender when pierced with a knife, about 20 minutes.

7. Serve the cauliflower steaks hot with the Walnut Sauce.

WALNUT SAUCE

½ cup (125 mL) raw walnut halves

2 tablespoons (30 mL) virgin olive oil, divided

1 small yellow onion, chopped

1 clove garlic, chopped

½ cup (125 mL) unsweetened almond milk

2 tablespoons (30 mL) fresh lemon juice

salt and pepper, to taste

SPICE-CRUSTED CAULIFLOWER

1 medium head of cauliflower

1 teaspoon (5 mL) sweet paprika

1 teaspoon (5 mL) minced fresh thyme leaves (about 2 sprigs)

Spaghetti Squash Noodle Bowls
with Lime Peanut Sauce

SERVES *4* FREE OF 🌿 🌾

This is far and away the most popular recipe from my blog. I think it appeals to the plant-eating crowd as well as to the low-carb-eating lovers out there, too. I take the natural, noodle-like strands of winter spaghetti squash and tangle them up into a whole meal with hearty greens, herbs, broccoli, and a delicious peanut sauce born out of pantry staples. It's a vibrant and clever way to enjoy heavier winter produce that looks and eats like a bowl of takeout noodles.

1. Preheat the oven to 375°F (190°C).

2. MAKE THE LIME PEANUT SAUCE: To a blender, add the ginger, garlic, hot sauce, peanut butter, lime, rice vinegar, agave nectar, tamari, grapeseed oil, salt, and pepper. Whiz on high until fully incorporated. Check the sauce for seasoning, adjust if necessary, and set aside.

3. PREPARE THE VEGETABLES: Line a baking sheet with parchment and place the squash halves, cut side down, onto the sheet. Bake for about 1 hour or until the flesh pulls away in easy strands. Remove from the oven and set aside to cool.

4. While the squash is baking, slice the kale leaves into thin ribbons and place in a large bowl.

5. Set a medium saucepan with about 1 inch (2.5 cm) of water over medium heat. Bring it to a simmer. Place the broccoli florets into a steamer basket and set aside.

6. When the squash is cool enough to handle, place the steamer basket of broccoli into the pot with the simmering water. Cover and allow the broccoli to steam until crisp-tender, about 4 minutes.

7. ASSEMBLE THE NOODLE BOWLS: While the broccoli is steaming, scrape the spaghetti squash strands out of the shell with a fork and into the bowl with the kale. The heat from the squash should wilt the kale slightly. Season the squash and kale with salt and pepper. Pour a big splash of Lime Peanut Sauce into the bowl, and toss to combine.

8. Remove the broccoli from the steamer. Portion the squash and kale into 4 bowls. Top each bowl with the steamed broccoli, sliced red onions, chopped cashews, sesame seeds, chopped cilantro, and extra Lime Peanut Sauce.

LIME PEANUT SAUCE

½-inch (1 cm) piece fresh ginger, peeled and chopped

2 cloves garlic, chopped

hot sauce, to taste

2 tablespoons (30 mL) natural peanut butter

1 lime, peeled and chopped

1 tablespoon (15 mL) unseasoned rice vinegar

2 teaspoons (10 mL) raw agave nectar

1 tablespoon (15 mL) gluten-free tamari soy sauce

⅓ cup (75 mL) grapeseed or other neutral-flavored oil

salt and pepper, to taste

NOODLE BOWLS

1 large spaghetti squash, cut in half lengthwise, seeds scooped out

6 curly kale leaves, stems removed

4 cups (1 L) broccoli florets (from 1 small bunch)

salt and pepper, to taste

½ small red onion, thinly sliced

½ cup (125 mL) toasted cashews, chopped

2 tablespoons (30 mL) sesame seeds

½ cup (125 mL) chopped fresh cilantro leaves

Burrito-Stuffed Sweet Potatoes
with Rustic Salsa

SERVES *4* FREE OF 🌿 🥜 🍚

I rarely eat burritos in their proper, wrapped-up package anymore. Throwing all the components into a bowl is so much easier to eat and involves a lot less effort. Add to this my love of baked and stuffed sweet potatoes, and you have the inspiration for this dish. While the sweet potatoes roast, you have ample time to fix all the filling components: some spiced beans and rice, a rustic salsa, and guacamole.

1. Preheat the oven to 400°F (200°C). Line a baking dish with parchment paper.

2. Place the sweet potatoes in the baking dish, and prick each one a couple of times with a fork. Slide the sweet potatoes into the oven and bake until very tender, about 45 minutes.

3. In a medium saucepan, combine the basmati rice, black beans, cumin, garlic, olive oil, tomato paste, and salt. Pour 1¼ cups (300 mL) water into the pot. Cover and bring to a boil over medium heat. Lower the heat to a simmer, and cook until all of the liquid is absorbed, about 40 minutes. Keep the rice warm.

4. MAKE THE RUSTIC SALSA: In a medium bowl, combine the bell pepper, cherry tomatoes, red onions, lime juice, cilantro, and olive oil. Season the mixture with salt and pepper, and toss to combine. Set aside.

5. MAKE THE GUACAMOLE: Peel the avocado and extract the pit. Place the avocado flesh in a medium bowl and mash with a fork. Once you've broken it up a bit, add the garlic, lime juice, cilantro, and salt. Mash the avocado until the seasoning is evenly distributed and you have a chunky paste. Set aside.

6. Place each baked sweet potato in a shallow bowl. Cut along the top of the sweet potato and pull back the skin. Split the sweet potatoes a little bit to make room for the fillings.

7. Divide the rice and bean mixture among the sweet potatoes. Top each bowl with ¼ of the Rustic Salsa. Finish each plate with a dollop of the guacamole and some shredded cabbage on top. Serve with hot sauce on the side if you like.

4 small sweet potatoes

½ cup (125 mL) uncooked brown basmati rice, rinsed

1 cup (250 mL) cooked black beans

1 teaspoon (5 mL) ground cumin

½ clove garlic, minced

½ teaspoon (2 mL) virgin olive oil

1 teaspoon (5 mL) tomato paste

pinch of salt

RUSTIC SALSA

1 yellow or red bell pepper, seeded and chopped

1 cup (250 mL) cherry tomatoes, halved

½ small red onion, chopped

1 tablespoon (15 mL) fresh lime juice

2 tablespoons (30 mL) chopped fresh cilantro leaves

1½ teaspoons (7 mL) virgin olive oil

salt and pepper, to taste

GUACAMOLE

1 ripe, medium-sized avocado

½ clove garlic, minced

1 tablespoon (15 mL) fresh lime juice

2 tablespoons (30 mL) chopped fresh cilantro leaves

generous pinch of salt

FOR SERVING

shredded cabbage OR romaine lettuce

hot sauce (optional)

French Onion Lentil Pots *with* Onion Cream Toasts

SERVES *4*   FREE OF 🥣

I bake these like a pot pie, with all of those familiar French onion flavors but thickened and made main-course appropriate with lentils. Everyone knows that the best part of eating French onion soup is the cheesy toast that accompanies the bowl. Instead of going the fake cheese route, I make a delicious and rich vegan cream out of some of the cooked-down onions. I add a pinch of nutritional yeast to make it really savory and it does the trick every time.

1. In a large soup pot, heat 2 tablespoons (30 mL) of the olive oil over medium heat. Add the sliced onions to the pot. You should hear a decent sizzle. Sauté until the onions are just starting to soften, about 3 minutes. Lower the heat. Slowly cook the onions until they are light brown, slightly jammy, and sweet, stirring frequently. This should take about 40 minutes. Add a splash of water to the pot if the onions start to dry up or burn.

2. Scoop ⅓ cup (75 mL) of the cooked onions out of the pot and set aside.

3. Increase the heat back to medium. Add the thyme, bay leaf, lentils, and tomato paste to the pot. Stir to combine. Add the balsamic vinegar and tamari, and use your spoon to scrape up any browned bits from the bottom of the pot. Season the mixture with salt and pepper, and then add the vegetable stock. Cover and bring to a boil. Lower the heat to a simmer, and cook until the lentils are tender, about 20 to 25 minutes.

4. Remove the bay leaf from the pot and discard. Divide the French onion lentil stew among four 1-cup (250 mL) ramekins. Place the filled ramekins on a baking sheet.

5. Preheat the broiler to high.

6. In a blender, combine the reserved cooked onions, remaining 1 teaspoon (5 mL) of olive oil, nutritional yeast, almond milk, salt, and pepper. Whiz on high until you have a chunky paste.

7. Spread the onion cream thinly over the baguette slices. Place 2 baguette slices over each pot of lentils.

8. Slide the French onion lentil pots under the broiler, and cook until the edges of the bread are crisp and browned, about 1 minute. Serve hot.

2 tablespoons + 1 teaspoon (30 mL + 5 mL) virgin olive oil, divided

2 pounds (1 kg) yellow onions, sliced

2 teaspoons (10 mL) minced fresh thyme leaves (about 4 sprigs)

1 bay leaf

1 cup (250 mL) French or black beluga lentils

1 tablespoon (15 mL) tomato paste

1 tablespoon (15 mL) balsamic vinegar

1 tablespoon (15 mL) gluten-free tamari soy sauce

salt and pepper, to taste

4 cups (1 L) vegetable stock

1 teaspoon (5 mL) nutritional yeast

¼ cup (50 mL) unsweetened almond milk

8 thin slices of whole-grain baguette (gluten-free if required)

Vegetables
& a Couple
of grains

Not quite main courses, and not quite salads or any other category of recipe: these dishes round out the table or serve as batch-cooked items to have on hand for a week of meals. Some of the options here are quite hearty in their own right, like the Fennel and Cherry Tomato Gratin (page 178) or the Garlicky Winter Vegetable and White Bean Mash with Mushroom Miso Gravy (page 183), and would do well served alongside a simple green salad. This category of food has always been my savior at large family dinners and other occasions when animal proteins are the center of the meal/the occasion itself. So I've tried to offer some thoughtful and streamlined options here for filling out your plate or throwing into the mix with other leftovers for a great weekday lunch.

Roasted Balsamic Beets

SERVES 6 FREE OF

I make batches of these sticky and sweet roasted beets all year to add to salads, to make as a beet salad outright, or to reheat as part of a larger pan of roasted vegetables. I think a lot of people have these negative associations with beets because of those crazy-sweet pickled ones in the jars. These ones have a gentle sweetness that's nicely balanced with the tart smack of balsamic vinegar. They're mind-changing, if you ask me.

1. Preheat the oven to 400°F (200°C).

2. Trim both ends of the beets and peel them. Cut the beets into ½-inch (1 cm) dices. Arrange the diced beets in a single layer in a large glass baking dish.

3. Drizzle the diced beets with ¼ cup (50 mL) of the balsamic vinegar, the maple syrup, and the olive oil. Season the beets with salt and pepper, and gently toss them until they're evenly coated. Cover the dish with foil and place in the oven.

4. Roast the covered beets for 25 minutes. Then, remove them from the oven and add the remaining 2 tablespoons (30 mL) of the balsamic vinegar. Carefully toss the beets to coat. Roast the beets uncovered for another 25 minutes or until fork-tender.

5. Serve beets immediately or allow them to cool thoroughly on the counter. Beets can be stored in a sealed container in the refrigerator for up to 5 days.

6 medium beets (any color), scrubbed

¼ cup + 2 tablespoons (50 mL + 30 mL) balsamic vinegar, divided

2 teaspoons (10 mL) pure maple syrup

1½ tablespoons (22 mL) virgin olive oil

salt and pepper, to taste

Crispy Salt and Vinegar Potatoes
with Lemon Garlic "Aioli"

SERVES *4*   FREE OF 🌿 🥣   REQUIRES *time to soak*

If I'm treating myself to a salty snack with a drink or maybe just a night on the couch with a movie, my preference will always be salt and vinegar potato chips. I like all manners of chips and potato snacks, but simply salted or salt and vinegar flavors are my go-tos. Maybe that's boring, but they are classics for a reason.

This starchy side hits all those pleasure points for me with an extra creamy bonus of garlicky pine nut mayonnaise for drizzling. If you roast them until very crispy—a little longer than specified—they make an excellent handheld dipping snack.

1. Preheat the oven to 400°F (200°C). Line a large baking sheet with parchment paper and set aside.

2. MAKE THE LEMON GARLIC "AIOLI": Place the pine nuts, filtered water, lemon juice, apple cider vinegar, olive oil, garlic, Dijon mustard, and sea salt in a high-speed blender. Mix on high until you have a smooth and creamy consistency, stopping the blender and scraping the sides down a couple of times if necessary. When it's ready, scoop the aioli into a small bowl, cover it with plastic wrap, and place in the fridge. The aioli should firm up quite a bit.

2. PREPARE THE POTATOES: Place the potatoes in a medium saucepan and cover with the white wine vinegar and filtered water. Over medium-high heat, bring to a boil, then reduce the heat and simmer until the potatoes are just tender, about 17 minutes. Drain the potatoes and lightly dry them with a kitchen towel.

3. Space the potatoes out on the prepared baking sheet. Once they are cool enough to handle, lightly flatten each potato with your hand. You don't want too much of the potato flesh to squeeze out.

4. Lightly brush the potatoes with half of the olive oil and sprinkle them with sea salt. Slide the baking sheet into the oven, and roast the potatoes for 12 minutes. Remove from the oven, flip the potatoes over, and brush with the remaining olive oil. Slide the baking sheet back into the oven, and roast for another 12 minutes or until the potatoes are browned and crispy on the edges.

5. Serve the potatoes hot with the Lemon Garlic "Aioli" on the side. Sprinkle with minced chives if you like.

LEMON GARLIC "AIOLI"

½ cup (125 mL) raw pine nuts, soaked at least 2 hours

3 tablespoons (45 mL) filtered water

1 tablespoon (15 mL) fresh lemon juice

1 teaspoon (5 mL) apple cider vinegar

1 tablespoon (15 mL) virgin olive oil

1 small clove garlic, minced

½ teaspoon (2 mL) Dijon mustard

pinch of fine sea salt

POTATOES

1 pound (454 g) mini waxy potatoes (I prefer Yukon golds)

1½ cups (375 mL) white wine vinegar

1½ cups (375 mL) filtered water

1 tablespoon (15 mL) virgin olive oil

sea salt, to taste

minced chives, for garnish (optional)

Fennel and Cherry Tomato Gratin

SERVES *6* FREE OF 🌿 🍚

Aside from shaving fresh fennel very thin for salads, fixing a gratin is my preferred preparation method for fennel (and for plenty of other vegetables). A crunchy topping with toasted walnuts is the perfect match for tender wedges of fennel baked with thyme and a splash of white wine. It's a simple assembly with elegant payoff. The topping is simply blitzed-up nuts with spices. You could easily make a nut-free version with an equal amount of sunflower or pumpkin seeds if you like.

1. Preheat the oven to 375°F (190°C).

2. Cut the fennel bulbs into 2-inch (5 cm) wedges, removing pieces of the core as you go. Arrange the fennel wedges facing up in a 13- × 9-inch (3 L) glass or metal baking dish.

3. Place the tomatoes in the crevices between the fennel wedges in the pan. Carefully pour the vegetable stock and white wine into the pan so that they distribute themselves evenly. Carefully drizzle the olive oil over the fennel wedges. Season the fennel with the minced thyme, salt, and pepper. Cover the dish tightly with foil, and bake in the oven for 35 minutes.

4. MAKE THE TOPPING: In the bowl of a food processor, combine the pine nuts, walnut halves, olive oil, nutritional yeast, garlic powder, and minced thyme. Pulse until you have a crumbly topping that holds together in small chunks.

5. After baking for 35 minutes, remove the fennel from the oven. Remove the foil, and sprinkle the topping all over the surface. Slide the gratin back into the oven and bake, uncovered, for another 20 minutes or until the topping is golden brown and the fennel is fork-tender. Serve the gratin hot.

2 fennel bulbs, long fronds and top stalks trimmed off

1 cup (250 mL) whole cherry tomatoes

⅓ cup (75 mL) vegetable stock

2 tablespoons (30 mL) dry white wine

1 tablespoon (15 mL) virgin olive oil

2 teaspoons (10 mL) minced fresh thyme leaves (about 4 sprigs)

salt and pepper, to taste

TOPPING

½ cup (125 mL) raw pine nuts

½ cup (125 mL) raw walnut halves

1 tablespoon (15 mL) virgin olive oil

1 tablespoon (15 mL) nutritional yeast

½ teaspoon (2 mL) garlic powder

2 teaspoons (10 mL) minced fresh thyme leaves (about 4 sprigs)

Roasted Cauliflower *with* Green Tahini

SERVES *4 as a side*   FREE OF 🌿 🥜 🌾

A plate I enjoyed with friends at an incredible Israeli restaurant in Philadelphia inspired this recipe. Before we enjoyed meaty chunks of eggplant cooked over coals and after we voraciously ate up plates of *salatim*, there was a dish of crispy fried cauliflower with a deep-green, tahini-based sauce on the side. The cauliflower, in all its fried glory, was the perfect foil to the creamy and fresh-tasting sauce. It took every bit of the restraint I had not to greedily scoop all of it up for myself. I knew I could make a non-fried version at home that was just as satisfying, as long as I could nail the sauce. This recipe is pretty close.

1. Preheat the oven to 400°F (200°C). Line a baking sheet with parchment paper.

2. Place the cauliflower florets and chickpeas on the baking sheet. Drizzle with the olive oil and lemon juice, and season with the za'atar spice, salt, and pepper. Toss the vegetables and chickpeas to coat.

3. Slide the baking sheet into the oven, and roast for 20 to 25 minutes, tossing the vegetables and chickpeas frequently. The chickpeas should be crisp and the cauliflower quite browned.

4. WHILE THE VEGETABLES ARE ROASTING, MAKE THE GREEN TAHINI: In a blender, combine the tahini, lemon juice, apple cider vinegar, filtered water, agave nectar, basil, green onions, garlic, salt, and pepper. Blend on high until it has a smooth, creamy texture. Add more filtered water if needed to make the dressing pourable. Check the seasonings and adjust if necessary.

5. Serve the caramelized cauliflower and chickpeas hot with the Green Tahini drizzled over top and some fresh lemon wedges on the side, if you like.

5 cups (1.25 L) small cauliflower florets (about 1 small head)

1 cup (250 mL) cooked chickpeas

1 tablespoon (15 mL) virgin olive oil

2 teaspoons (10 mL) fresh lemon juice

2 teaspoons (10 mL) za'atar spice

salt and pepper, to taste

GREEN TAHINI (*makes extra*)

⅓ cup (75 mL) tahini

2 tablespoons (30 mL) fresh lemon juice

2 teaspoons (10 mL) apple cider vinegar

2 tablespoons (30 mL) filtered water, plus extra (depending on thickness of tahini)

1 tablespoon (15 mL) raw agave nectar OR pure maple syrup

½ cup (125 mL) fresh basil leaves

4 green onions, chopped

1 clove garlic, chopped

salt and pepper, to taste

FOR SERVING

fresh lemon wedges (optional)

Garlicky Winter Vegetable and White Bean Mash *with* Mushroom Miso Gravy

SERVES *4* FREE OF 🌿 🍚

This recipe has all of the comfort of the classic mashed potatoes and gravy combination, but none of the leaden stomach feeling afterward. The mix of white winter vegetables adds a healthy dose of vitamins, plus a more interesting flavor profile, with all of the fluff and lightness of traditional mashed potatoes. I mash cooked white beans in with the vegetables for some extra protein, but you could just increase the amount of vegetables if you don't have any on hand. The gravy tastes delicious on almost anything you could think of, so don't limit yourself by only making it for this recipe.

1. MAKE THE VEGETABLE AND BEAN MASH: Place the diced celery root, cauliflower, parsnips, and garlic cloves in a medium saucepan. Cover the vegetables with cold water and then place the pot over medium heat. Bring to a boil and then simmer until the vegetables are tender, about 15 minutes.

2. Drain the vegetables and place them in the bowl of a food processor along with the white beans. Pulse the vegetables and beans a couple of times to lightly chop them. Add the almond milk, olive oil, salt, and pepper. Run the motor on high speed until you have a creamy and smooth mixture. Keep it warm.

3. MAKE THE MUSHROM MISO GRAVY: Heat the olive oil in a large sauté pan over medium heat. Add the mushrooms, and let them sit for 2 full minutes. Stir them up and let them sear for another full minute. Add the thyme and garlic, and stir. After the mushrooms start to glisten slightly, season them with salt and pepper. Add the balsamic vinegar and stir.

4. In a small bowl, whisk together the vegetable stock, miso, and arrowroot powder until no lumps of miso remain. Pour this mixture into the pan with the mushrooms, and stir.

5. Bring the gravy to a light simmer, and cook until the gravy has thickened slightly.

6. Serve the Mushroom Miso Gravy piping hot on top of the vegetable mash. Sprinkle with freshly ground black pepper if you like.

VEGETABLE AND BEAN MASH

2 cups (500 mL) peeled and diced celery root (from 1 medium-sized celery root)

2 cups (500 mL) chopped cauliflower

1 cup (250 mL) chopped parsnips (from 2 medium parsnips)

5 cloves garlic, peeled

1 cup (250 mL) cooked and drained white beans, such as navy or cannellini

¾ cup (175 mL) unsweetened almond milk

1 teaspoon (5 mL) virgin olive oil

salt and pepper, to taste

MUSHROOM MISO GRAVY

1 tablespoon (15 mL) virgin olive oil

5 cups (1.25 L) sliced mushrooms (I like cremini or shiitake)

2 teaspoons (10 mL) chopped fresh thyme leaves (about 4 sprigs)

4 cloves garlic, minced

salt and pepper, to taste

2 teaspoons (10 mL) balsamic vinegar

1¼ cups (300 mL) vegetable stock

1 tablespoon (15 mL) mellow or light miso

2 teaspoons (10 mL) arrowroot powder

freshly ground black pepper, for serving (optional)

Fancy Rice

SERVES *4*   FREE OF 🌿 🍚

I make this every time I have family over, and I add some finely diced seasonal fruit: apples in the fall, blood oranges in the winter, strawberries in the spring, and plums or other stone fruit in the summer. Most people enjoy rice, and a beautifully herb-flecked bowl of it with fruit, crunchy nuts, and spice is hard to resist. The sumac is an unusual addition, but its sour, earthy flavor plays well here. You could substitute any ground spice you happen to love.

1. Place the wild and brown rice blend in a medium saucepan. Cover the rice with cold water by 1 inch (2.5 cm). Bring to a boil, lower the heat to a simmer, and cover. Cook the rice for 40 minutes or until all the liquid is absorbed. Remove from the heat and let the rice sit for 5 minutes. Fluff the rice with a fork, and gently transfer it to a medium bowl.

2. Add the olive oil, apple cider vinegar, coriander, sumac, dried cranberries, parsley, green onions, salt, and pepper to the rice. Toss gently to combine. Garnish the rice with the chopped almonds. Serve warm.

1 cup (250 mL) uncooked wild and brown rice blend, rinsed

2 teaspoons (10 mL) virgin olive oil

1 teaspoon (5 mL) apple cider vinegar

½ teaspoon (2 mL) ground coriander

¼ teaspoon (1 mL) ground sumac

¼ cup (50 mL) unsweetened dried cranberries

¼ cup (50 mL) chopped fresh flat-leaf parsley

2 green onions, thinly sliced

salt and pepper, to taste

¼ cup (50 mL) almonds, chopped, for garnish

Roasted Carrots
with Ginger Maple Cream

SERVES *4 to 6*   FREE OF 🌿 🥜

I used to love the sugar-glazed carrots side dish when I was a kid, and this preparation feels like a more grown-up, health-considerate version of it. One mouthful is spicy, citrusy, sweet, and creamy, which is side dish heaven as far as I'm concerned. Sometimes I spread the ginger maple cream out on the plate so that the carrots can be swiped through, and other times I like to drizzle it right on top for a more dramatic presentation.

1. Preheat the oven to 400°F (200°C). Line a baking sheet with parchment paper.

2. PREPARE THE CARROTS: Place the carrots on the baking sheet. Toss them with the thyme, olive oil, salt, and pepper. Arrange the carrots in a single layer, and slide the baking sheet into the oven. Roast the carrots until just tender, about 25 minutes. Flip and toss the carrots at the halfway mark.

3. MAKE THE GINGER MAPLE CREAM: In a medium bowl, stir the cashew butter with the water until no big chunks of cashew butter remain. Press the cashew butter on the side of the bowl and slowly work it into the water. Whisk in the maple syrup, lemon juice, and grated ginger. Season the cream with salt.

4. Arrange the carrots on a serving platter. Drizzle the Ginger Maple Cream over the carrots, and serve warm.

CARROTS

1 pound (454 g) medium carrots, cut into ½-inch (1 cm) batons

1 teaspoon (5 mL) minced fresh thyme leaves (about 2 sprigs)

2 teaspoons (10 mL) virgin olive oil

salt and pepper, to taste

GINGER MAPLE CREAM

2 tablespoons (30 mL) raw cashew butter

1½ tablespoons (22 mL) filtered water

1 tablespoon (15 mL) pure maple syrup

1½ teaspoons (7 mL) fresh lemon juice

1-inch (2.5 cm) piece of fresh ginger, peeled and finely grated with a Microplane grater

salt, to taste

Miso Millet "Polenta" *with* Green Onions

SERVES *2 to 4*   FREE OF 🌿 🥜 🍚

Who knew that ground millet could make a beautiful and fluffy alternative polenta? This forms a beautiful base for roasted vegetables or stewed beans. For a topping, I steep some chopped green onions in hot grapeseed oil before giving it all a blend, and it makes the most brilliant green finish. The mellow creaminess of this side is an especially perfect foil to all kinds of spring vegetables.

⅓ cup + 2 teaspoons (75 mL + 10 mL) grapeseed or other heat-tolerant oil, divided

½ cup (125 mL) green onions, white and green parts, chopped, plus extra for garnish

generous pinch of salt

1 cup (250 mL) millet

2 leeks, white and light-green parts only, chopped

3 cups (750 mL) vegetable stock

2 teaspoons (10 mL) mellow or light miso

1. Heat the ⅓ cup (75 mL) of grapeseed oil in a medium saucepan over medium heat. When the oil starts shimmering or rippling, it should be hot enough. Carefully transfer the chopped green onions to the oil. Let them sizzle and fry until they turn bright green and fragrant, about 15 to 20 seconds.

2. Carefully transfer the oil and green onions to a blender. Add a fat pinch of salt and blend until the oil appears creamy and green with no visible chunks of green onion. Set aside.

3. In a food processor or blender, grind the millet until the texture resembles coarse flour. Set aside.

4. Return the saucepan to the stove over medium heat with the remaining 2 teaspoons (10 mL) of oil. Add the leeks and stir. Cook until the leeks are quite tender, about 5 minutes. Add the vegetable stock and miso to the pan, and bring to a boil. Slowly sprinkle in the ground millet flour while whisking. Keep whisking the ground millet and stock until you have a thick, cooked, polenta-like mixture.

5. Serve the millet polenta hot with drizzles of the green onion oil (there will be extra—store remainder in a sealed jar in the refrigerator for up to 1 week) and chopped green onions on top.

Spring Steamed Vegetables
with Savory Goji Berry Cream

SERVES *4 to 6*   FREE OF 🌿 🌾

I had a giant bag of dried goji berries in my pantry and had been struggling to find ways to use them. Most of them went into my daily smoothie, but I couldn't help feeling that I was neglecting their potential by using them up this way. Their slightly woodsy flavor was getting buried in all the fruit and other add-ins. I started thinking that they would make a beautiful base for a savory sauce. Soaked dried fruit becomes surprisingly creamy once it's blended, and this sauce is no exception. I love massaging it into raw kale with some extra fresh lemon juice for a delicious and unusual salad.

1. MAKE THE SAVORY GOJI BERRY CREAM: Place the goji berries in a small bowl and cover them with boiling water. Let the berries sit for 5 minutes or until they've plumped and softened. Spoon the goji berries into a blender, reserving the soaking water.

2. Add the apple cider vinegar, miso, lemon juice, ginger, maple syrup, olive oil, salt, and pepper to the blender. Add 3 tablespoons (45 mL) of the goji soaking water, and then whiz the mixture on high until creamy and smooth. Set aside.

3. STEAM THE VEGETABLES: After you've trimmed the vegetables, set a large pot with about 1 inch (2.5 cm) of water on the stove. Bring the water to a simmer. Arrange the vegetables in a steamer basket and set them into the pot. Cover and steam until all the vegetables are just tender, about 8 minutes.

4. Arrange the steamed vegetables on your serving platter and top with the Savory Goji Berry Cream. Garnish with the chopped walnuts and sliced green onions.

SAVORY GOJI BERRY CREAM

¼ cup (50 mL) dried goji berries

1 tablespoon (15 mL) apple cider vinegar

1 tablespoon (15 mL) mellow or light miso

1 tablespoon (15 mL) fresh lemon juice

1-inch (2.5 cm) piece of fresh ginger, peeled and chopped

1 teaspoon (5 mL) pure maple syrup

3 tablespoons (45 mL) virgin olive oil

salt and pepper, to taste

VEGETABLES

1½ pounds (681 g) trimmed spring vegetables (I like halved baby carrots, asparagus, and quartered radishes)

salt and pepper, to taste

GARNISHES

scant ¼ cup (50 mL) walnut halves, toasted and chopped

1 green onion, thinly sliced

Glowing, Fermented Vegetable Tangle

MAKES *about 2 quarts (2 L)*　FREE OF 🌿 🥜 🌶 🥣
REQUIRES *time to ferment*

When I lived in Toronto, I got hooked on this turmeric-stained fermented salad from a stand at one of the farmers' markets. Before trying that salad, I had only experienced fermented vegetables in the form of traditional kimchi and sauerkraut. This salad had apples and all kinds of vegetables in the mix, as well as little pops of whole spices. I started putting it on everything and found myself buying it every few weeks. After doing some internet research on home fermentation, I found out that making this sort of thing wasn't that hard as long as you had patience and kept an eye on things.

1. Over a large bowl, shave the fennel very thinly with a mandoline. Then shave the cabbage with the mandoline over the same bowl.

2. Add the carrots, beets, apples, ginger, turmeric, cumin seeds, and chili flakes to the bowl. Season everything liberally with sea salt. Massage the vegetables for a solid 5 minutes or until a good amount of liquid pools at the bottom of the bowl. Wear gloves to avoid turmeric-stained hands.

3. Pack the vegetables into jars with tight-fitting lids, pressing down with your hands or a spatula so that the liquid seeps up and covers the surface. Leave 1 inch (2.5 cm) empty at the top of the jar. Press a flexible, outer cabbage leaf onto the top of each jar of mixture, and press down once more. Secure the lid on each jar.

4. Since the liquid in this can stain, I like to further secure the jars in plastic bags with knots tied at the top. Place the bagged jars in a large bowl somewhere out of the way. I keep mine in the basement. Make a note on your calendar to check the jars in 3 weeks. The vegetables should taste lightly sour and tangy, and should have a little texture when you bite down.

5. If the vegetables are to your liking, remove the cabbage leaf toppers and store the jars in the refrigerator.

1 fennel bulb, cored

1 head green cabbage, quartered and cored (save the flexible outer leaves)

6 medium carrots, shredded

2 medium beets (I like golden ones for this), shredded

2 apples, peeled, cored and shredded

2-inch (5 cm) piece of fresh ginger, peeled and finely grated with a Microplane grater

2-inch (5 cm) piece of fresh turmeric root, peeled and finely grated with a Microplane grater OR 2 teaspoons (10 mL) turmeric powder

2 teaspoons (10 mL) cumin seeds

2 teaspoons (10 mL) chili flakes

sea salt, to taste

Crispy Maple Mustard Cabbage

SERVES *4 to 6*   FREE OF 🌿 🥜 🌰

The appeal of this side dish is not surprising with the grainy pops of mustard punctuating the whole experience. The cabbage gets so sweet, and the crispy edges make it crave-worthy. I find cabbage to be an underrated ingredient in general, so this preparation is most welcome in the depths of winter when I'm starting to run out of vegetable inspiration.

1. Preheat the oven to 400°F (200°C).

2. In a small bowl, whisk together the olive oil, grainy mustard, and maple syrup.

3. Cut the cabbage into 1-inch (2.5 cm) wedges. Once you have the wedges, remove most of the core, leaving a thin strip intact so that the wedge holds together through the roasting process.

4. Lay the wedges on a large baking sheet. Brush the side facing up with the olive oil mixture. Season with salt and pepper. Slide the baking sheet into the oven, and roast for 20 minutes.

5. Remove the baking sheet from the oven, and carefully flip the wedges over with a spatula. Brush with the remaining olive oil mixture. Slide the baking sheet back into the oven, and roast for another 20 minutes or until the cabbage wedges are quite browned and have crispy edges. Serve the cabbage warm.

2 tablespoons (30 mL) virgin olive oil

1 tablespoon (15 mL) grainy mustard

1½ teaspoons (7 mL) pure maple syrup

½ head large cabbage OR 1 small whole cabbage

salt and pepper, to taste

Red Peppers *with* Herby Breadcrumbs

SERVES *4 to 6*   FREE OF 🫑 🥖

The simplest preparations often have the largest reward. Tender, sweet, well-seasoned summer peppers with a shower of crunchy breadcrumbs are a win every time. Crispy starch (in any form) is delicious with almost anything. If you're grilling other items outside, cooking the peppers on the grill for a lightly smoky flavor is a great option, too. I make these herby breadcrumbs for all kinds of cooked vegetables and pasta dishes since I usually have leftover bread to use up.

4 red bell peppers, cores and stems removed

3 tablespoons (45 mL) virgin olive oil, divided

salt and pepper, to taste

2½ cups (625 mL) cubed stale bread

2 teaspoons (10 mL) minced fresh thyme leaves (about 4 sprigs)

1 clove garlic, minced

½ teaspoon (2 mL) fresh lemon zest

¼ teaspoon (1 mL) nutritional yeast

¼ cup (50 mL) chopped fresh flat-leaf parsley

1. Preheat the oven to 400°F (200°C). Line a baking sheet with parchment paper.

2. Cut each bell pepper into 4 segments. Remove any white pith pieces from the center, and place them on the baking sheet. Toss the bell peppers with 1 tablespoon (15 mL) of the olive oil. Spread the peppers out into a single layer, and season with salt and pepper. Slide the peppers into the oven, and roast until just tender, about 25 minutes.

3. Place the cubed bread into a food processor, and pulse the machine to make coarse crumbs.

4. Heat the remaining 2 tablespoons (30 mL) of the olive oil in a medium sauté pan over medium heat. Add the breadcrumbs to the pan along with some salt and pepper. Cook the breadcrumbs, stirring frequently, until evenly golden brown, about 10 minutes. Add the thyme, garlic, lemon zest, and nutritional yeast, and cook until fragrant, about 30 seconds.

5. Remove the breadcrumbs from the heat, and stir in the chopped parsley.

6. Arrange the roasted peppers on a platter and shower with the warm breadcrumbs. Serve warm.

Energizing
Drinks
&
Small Bites

These recipes make up the in-between bits of the day, and they serve as little, unusual bites to get a party started as well. None of these recipes are terribly fussy, favoring a more rustic approach so that you can spend more time socializing. In this section, I also include some easy and delicious recipes for pantry staples like crackers and granola bars that will steer you away from the store-bought versions for life. I include drinks here, but I could have devoted an entire book to them, if I'm being honest. When you're trying to get your bearings on a healthy, plant-based lifestyle, mastering a few wellness drinks can really help clean up some less-than-perfect habits. I've included some tonic-like refreshers and my go-to green smoothie combination in this chapter to keep you hydrated and nourished throughout the day.

Salted Caramel Date Shake

SERVES *2*   FREE OF 🌿 🥜 💧 🥥

This is like drinking salted caramel ice cream, except the ingredients make it perfectly suitable for the breakfast hour (I generally prefer sweet things for breakfast, so there's that to consider). It's almost too good. Soaking the sugary-sweet dates guarantees optimum blending if you don't have a high-speed blender. If you have access to very fresh dates, you can skip that step. I quite like the amount of salt here, but if you are unsure, start with a tiny pinch and work up if necessary.

5 Medjool dates, pitted

¾ cup (175 mL) full-fat coconut milk

1 teaspoon (5 mL) pure vanilla extract

¼ teaspoon (1 mL) sea salt

½ teaspoon (2 mL) fresh lemon juice

1½ cups (375 mL) ice

1. If your dates are fudgy-soft, you can skip this step. Place the pitted dates in a small bowl and cover them with boiling water. Let the dates soak for 5 minutes.

2. Strain the dates and place them in a high-speed blender. Add the coconut milk, vanilla, sea salt, lemon juice, and ice.

3. Blend the mixture on high until the ice is uniformly crushed throughout the liquid and you have a smooth, milkshake-like texture. Pour into 2 glasses, and drink immediately.

A Casually Specific Green Smoothie

SERVES *1 to 2 (meal size or snack)*   FREE OF 🌿 🥜 💧 🥥

I prefer my green smoothies to be water, coconut water, or juice based. I find the flavor of almond or other plant milks clashes with the fresh and vibrant nature of the greens. When I crave a green smoothie, I want bright fruit and vegetable-forward flavors. I still like to taste the greens, crazy as that sounds. This combination is my old reliable when that craving sets in. It's fresh, tart, lightly sweet, and undeniably green-tasting.

1. Place the coconut water, lime, greens, herbs, cucumbers, kiwis, and pineapple in a high-speed blender. Blend the mixture on high for 1 minute or until no visible chunks of greens remain.

2. Serve the smoothie cold.

1½ cups (375 mL) unsweetened coconut water

1 whole lime, peeled and chopped

1½ cups (375 mL) chopped greens (I prefer chard, spinach, or romaine lettuce leaves)

¼ cup (50 mL) fresh mixed herbs, such as parsley, cilantro, mint, and basil

½ English cucumber, chopped

2 kiwis, peeled and chopped

½ cup (125 mL) frozen pineapple OR mango

Hot-Pink Beet Protein Smoothie

SERVES *1*   FREE OF 🌿 💧 🥣

Among many other things, my dad grows beets in his garden. He delivers a decent variety of goods to a lot of family members and friends, but I'm the only one that likes beets, so I get all of them. I had to start coming up with a few new ways to consume them (see the Roasted Balsamic Beets on page 175 for my favorite savory recipe). This smoothie combination seems odd at first, but I promise you that it works. The earthy, lightly sweet beet mixes with tart berries, warm vanilla, and almond butter perfectly. And the color is irresistible. I usually have a freezer full of raspberries (also from Dad's garden), so I enjoy this smoothie at least three or four times a week.

1. Place the clementine, beet, red berries, banana, almond butter, chia seeds, almond milk, vanilla, and sea salt, if using, into a high-speed blender. Blend the mixture on high for 2 minutes, or until completely smooth.

2. Serve the smoothie cold.

1 juicy clementine OR tangerine, peeled and broken into segments

1 small beet, peeled and chopped

½ cup (125 mL) red berries of choice (such as raspberries or strawberries)

½ ripe banana, preferably frozen

2 tablespoons (30 mL) raw or roasted almond butter (I prefer roasted)

1 tablespoon (15 mL) chia seeds

1 cup (250 mL) unsweetened almond milk

¼ teaspoon (1 mL) pure vanilla extract

⅛ teaspoon (0.5 mL) fine sea salt (omit if using salted almond butter)

Matcha Chia Limeade

MAKES *4 cups (1 L)*   FREE OF 🌿🥜🍶🌾   REQUIRES *time for prep*

Chia fresca is a refreshing summer drink with plenty of citrus juice that can help you stay hydrated in the heat because of the chia seeds' natural ability to retain water. This version gets a little boost from matcha powder and extra lime. Deep-green heat relief!

1. In a medium saucepan over medium heat, bring 1 cup (250 mL) of the filtered water, syrup, and matcha to a light simmer. Whisk until no large lumps of matcha appear. Remove from the heat.

2. Pour the lime juice into a large pitcher. Add the remaining 2 cups (500 mL) filtered water, chia seeds and stir. Add the matcha mixture, and stir to combine.

3. Chill the limeade in the refrigerator for a couple of hours. This will give the chia seeds some time to gel. Stir the limeade before serving over plenty of ice.

3 cups (750 mL) filtered water, divided

¼ cup (50 mL) raw agave syrup

2 tablespoons (30 mL) matcha (green tea powder)

1 cup (250 mL) fresh lime juice

3 tablespoons (45 mL) chia seeds

ice, for serving

Turmeric Cider "Switchy"

MAKES *2 to 3 drinks*   FREE OF 🌿 🥜 💧 ✳️   REQUIRES *time for prep*

Switchel or "switchy" is an irresistibly old-fashioned health tonic that my brother introduced me to. The main components are fresh ginger, raw apple cider vinegar, and some type of liquid sweetener. I love the clean and revitalizing feel of an apple cider vinegar drink, and this particular one makes the experience of drinking vinegar quite tantalizing. I add freshly grated turmeric root to mine for the gorgeous color and warming properties. Canadian maple syrup is always my natural sweetener of choice, and it tastes perfect with the sharp ginger here. I like drinking this straight, but a splash of sparkling water is a nice effervescent touch.

1. Combine the grated ginger, grated turmeric, maple syrup, apple cider vinegar, filtered water, and vanilla powder, if using, in a jar with a tight-fitting lid. Secure the lid and give the mixture a good shake. Let it steep overnight in the refrigerator.

2. To serve, strain the switchel through a fine-mesh strainer, and drink either straight, with ice cubes, or topped up with sparkling water.

1-inch (2.5 cm) piece of fresh ginger, finely grated

1-inch (2.5 cm) piece of fresh turmeric, finely grated

2 tablespoons (30 mL) pure maple syrup

2 tablespoons + 1 teaspoon (30 mL + 5 mL) raw apple cider vinegar

1½ cups (375 mL) filtered water

¼ teaspoon (1 mL) vanilla powder (optional)

TO SERVE

ice (optional)

sparkling water (optional)

Overnight Iced Tea

MAKES *4 cups (1 L)*   FREE OF 🌿 🥜 💧 🌾   REQUIRES *time for prep*

Since you brew this tea in the refrigerator overnight, there's no real need to serve it "iced." I prefer this method to hot brewing because it extracts the flavor of a good loose-leaf tea in a gentler way, making it less likely to go bitter.

1. Place the tea and chopped fruit in a nonreactive pitcher or glass jar.

2. Cover the tea and fruit with the filtered water. Place the pitcher in the refrigerator, allowing the tea to steep overnight.

3. Strain the tea in the morning, discarding the tea leaves and fruit. Serve the tea straight up or over ice, with agave nectar stirred in if you like.

6 teaspoons loose-leaf tea of your choice OR 5 to 6 tea bags

chopped citrus OR other juicy fruit, such as berries or summer peaches

4 cups (1 L) filtered water

ice, for serving

raw agave nectar, to taste

Sunshine Everything Crackers

MAKES *about 60 1-inch (2.5 cm) crackers*   FREE OF

These golden crisp crackers remind me of those cheesy goldfish-shaped snacks that I used to love in my pre-vegan days. They're nice to have around for dips and appetizer platters. I mostly just snack on them plain because they have so much flavor. I cut them into boring old squares, but if you have some cute mini cutters or forms, you could have some fun with these.

1 cup (250 mL) chickpea flour

1 cup (250 mL) certified gluten-free oat flour

2 teaspoons (10 mL) nutritional yeast

1 teaspoon (5 mL) fine sea salt

2 teaspoons (10 mL) garlic powder

1 teaspoon (5 mL) ground turmeric

pinch of cayenne pepper (optional)

¼ cup + 2 tablespoons (50 mL + 30 mL) sunflower oil

¼ cup (50 mL) filtered water, plus extra, if necessary

¼ cup (50 mL) mixed raw seeds (sesame, sunflower, and hemp are my favorites)

1. Preheat the oven to 350°F (180°C).

2. In the bowl of a food processor, combine the chickpea flour, oat flour, nutritional yeast, sea salt, garlic powder, ground turmeric, cayenne pepper, if using, and sunflower oil. Pulse the machine to get everything lightly mixed. Mix on high until you have a wet and uniform crumbly mixture.

3. With the food processor on low, slowly pour the filtered water through the feed tube of the food processor. The cracker dough should start to form a large ball. If the ball isn't forming, add more water by the teaspoon through the feed tube.

4. Open the lid of the food processor and add the mixed seeds. Pulse the dough a couple of times to distribute the seeds.

5. Lay a sheet of parchment paper, about the size of a large baking sheet, on the counter. Dump the cracker dough onto the parchment and flatten it a bit with your hands. Lay another sheet of parchment paper on top of the dough.

6. With a rolling pin, evenly roll the cracker dough out to roughly an ⅛ inch (3 mm) thickness. Remove the top sheet of parchment paper. Carefully transfer the parchment with the rolled-out cracker dough to a large baking sheet.

7. With a knife, score the cracker dough into a grid, forming 1-inch (2.5 cm) square crackers. Slide the baking sheet into the oven and bake until the edges of the crackers have browned slightly, about 20 minutes. Let the crackers cool completely before storing in a sealed container. The crackers will keep for about 5 days.

Seedy Sesame Granola Bars *with* Chocolate

MAKES *16 to 18 bars*   FREE OF 🌿 🥜

I've made my share of homemade granola bars over the years, always going for that trifecta of chewy, crisp, and just sticky *enough* all in one go. These sesame-flecked bars are the only ones I make now. I've also made these with almond butter in place of the tahini with equally delicious results.

1. Preheat the oven to 350°F (180°C). Grease an 11- × 7-inch (2 L) pan with coconut oil. Line the pan with parchment paper, leaving an overhang on the two long sides. Rub more coconut oil onto the parchment paper. Set aside.

2. In a large bowl, combine the oats, sea salt, sunflower seeds, sesame seeds, cacao nibs, and chia seeds. Toss to evenly mix. Set aside.

3. In a medium saucepan over medium-low heat, combine the tahini, brown rice syrup, maple syrup, coconut oil, and vanilla. Gently heat the mixture, stirring constantly with a spatula. Do not simmer or boil the mixture. Just heat it until the mixture is slightly more fluid and totally homogeneous.

4. Pour the tahini and syrup mixture over the oats and seeds. Scrape everything out of the pot, and stir the granola bar mix together until thoroughly combined. It might get a bit stiff as the tahini syrup mixture cools.

5. Press the granola bar mixture into the prepared pan as firmly as you can. I find this easier to do if you cover your hand with plastic wrap and press down on the mixture as evenly as possible.

6. Bake the granola bars for 25 to 27 minutes or until the edges are slightly golden brown. Cool the pan completely on a wire rack before cutting into bars.

(recipe continues)

3½ cups (875 mL) certified gluten-free rolled oats (not quick-cooking oats)

1 teaspoon (5 mL) fine sea salt

1 cup (250 mL) raw sunflower seeds

⅓ cup (75 mL) sesame seeds

⅓ cup (75 mL) cacao nibs

⅓ cup (75 mL) chia seeds

⅔ cup (150 mL) tahini

⅔ cup (150 mL) brown rice syrup

⅓ cup (75 mL) pure maple syrup

1 tablespoon (15 mL) liquid refined coconut oil, plus extra for greasing the pan

2 teaspoons (10 mL) pure vanilla extract

⅓ cup (75 mL) vegan semi-sweet chocolate chips

7. In a medium saucepan over medium-low heat, bring about 1 inch (2.5 cm) of water to a simmer. Place the chocolate chips in a nonreactive bowl, and set it on top of the pot with the simmering water. Stir the chocolate until completely melted. Drizzle the chocolate over cooled and cut granola bars. Place the bars in the refrigerator to firm up the chocolate.

8. You can store the bars in a sealed container at room temperature for about 1 week. You can also freeze the bars by individually wrapping each one in plastic wrap as tightly as you can. I like to place all the individually wrapped bars into a big resealable freezer bag and defrost them as I need them.

Super Seeded Kale Crisps

MAKES *5 cups (1.25 L) of crisps*   FREE OF 🌿 🥜 🌾

These kale chips are extra crunchy because they get a delicious coating of chia, hemp, and sesame seeds. I like regular kale chips, but I find them sort of wimpy in comparison to more typical salty snacks. The seeds help bolster the crunch, and they add some toasty flavor as well. I prefer lacinato or flat kale for these because they dry out easier and therefore crisp much faster. It's important to bake these in a single layer to avoid soggy chips.

1 bunch lacinato or dino kale, cut into bite-sized pieces (about 6 cups/1.5 L packed chopped kale)

1 tablespoon (15 mL) virgin olive oil

1½ teaspoons (7 mL) pure maple syrup

½ teaspoon (2 mL) apple cider vinegar

¾ teaspoon (3 mL) chili powder

¼ cup (50 mL) mixed hemp, chia, and sesame seeds

salt and pepper, to taste

1. Preheat the oven to 400°F (200°C). Line a large baking sheet with parchment paper and set aside.

2. In a large bowl, toss the kale, olive oil, maple syrup, apple cider vinegar, chili powder, seed mixture, and salt and pepper together, massaging the seasoning and seeds into the kale leaves.

3. Spread the kale onto the large baking sheet in a single layer, with as little overlap as possible.

4. Bake the kale crisps for 7 to 8 minutes, rotating the sheet at the halfway point. The edges should be lightly browned and crisp. Some centers of the kale leaves may still appear wet, but they will crisp up as they cool.

5. Let crisps cool before eating. Store cooled kale crisps in a large resealable bag at room temperature.

Avocado Tartare

MAKES *2 cups (500 mL) of tartare*   FREE OF

I love an unexpected appetizer or snack and this one fits the bill nicely. I know that a vegan version of traditional beef tartare isn't exactly at the top of everyone's list, but the concept seems so right with avocado. The presentation is beautiful for guests, but the preparation is easy enough for snacking on during a quiet night in watching TV. It's about as much effort as guacamole but less predictable. All in one bite there's salt, tang, sweetness, and those light nudges of umami too. If I have the foresight, I like serving this on sturdy crackers with some small dices of my Roasted Balsamic Beets (page 175) for that satisfying tangy-creamy combination.

1. In a medium bowl, combine the diced red onion, capers, parsley, Dijon mustard, lemon juice, tamari, olive oil, salt, and pepper.

2. Cut the avocado down the middle and remove the pit. Carefully peel the exterior, trying to preserve the integrity of the flesh. Dice the flesh somewhat small and add it to the medium bowl. Toss everything to combine. Add the hot sauce, if using, and toss again. Check the tartare for seasoning and adjust accordingly.

3. Garnish with the extra chopped parsley. Serve the avocado tartare immediately with crackers or crostini.

¼ cup (50 mL) finely diced red onion

2 tablespoons (30 mL) capers, drained and minced

¼ cup (50 mL) minced fresh flat-leaf parsley, plus extra for garnish

1 teaspoon (5 mL) Dijon mustard

2 teaspoons (10 mL) fresh lemon juice

½ teaspoon (2 mL) gluten-free tamari soy sauce

1 teaspoon (5 mL) virgin olive oil

salt and pepper, to taste

1 medium just-ripe avocado

4 to 5 drops of hot sauce (optional)

crackers and crostini, for serving (gluten-free if required)

Cauliflower and Pine Nut "Ricotta" Toasts

MAKES *1½ cups (375 mL) of ricotta*   FREE OF 🌿 🍲
REQUIRES *time to soak*

This "ricotta" is so creamy, and it's all in the whipping of the steamed cauliflower with some olive oil. This spread is better suited to crostini with some seasonal fruit or preserves, rather than layering into lasagna or something similar. I especially love it with sliced, ripe figs and tiny drops of good balsamic vinegar.

1. Set up a steamer basket over a large pot of simmering water. Place the chopped cauliflower in the basket, and cover the pot with a tight-fitting lid. Let the cauliflower steam for 15 minutes, or until tender.

2. Remove the cauliflower from the pot, and carefully transfer the florets to the bowl of a food processor. To the cauliflower, add the thyme, pine nuts, olive oil, lemon zest, lemon juice, nutritional yeast, and sea salt.

3. Pulse a few times to break up the cauliflower and nuts. Then run on high until you have a smooth, almost purée-like texture. You may have to stop the food processor and scrape the bowl down a couple of times.

4. Scrape the ricotta into a small bowl, and cover it with plastic wrap. Chill for at least 30 minutes before serving with toasted baguette slices and fruit.

3 cups (750 mL) chopped cauliflower

1 teaspoon (5 mL) fresh thyme leaves (about 2 sprigs)

¼ cup (50 mL) raw pine nuts, soaked for at least 4 hours

2 tablespoons (30 mL) virgin olive oil

1 teaspoon (5 mL) lemon zest

1 tablespoon (15 mL) fresh lemon juice

½ teaspoon (2 mL) nutritional yeast

½ teaspoon (2 mL) sea salt

FOR SERVING

toasted baguette slices (gluten-free if required)

fruit

good quality balsamic vinegar

Mustard-Roasted Broccoli Pâté

MAKES *2 cups (500 mL) of pâté*   FREE OF 🌿 🥜 🥣

REQUIRES *time for prep*

A board of pickled vegetables, dips, crackers, crostini, olives, and the like is a meal at our house often enough. It's a nice kitchen clean-out for the half-used containers of hummus and stale bread that sometimes pile up. I make this pâté when we have some broccoli that might be starting to wilt in the crisper. Roasting it intensifies the sweet flavor, and blitzing it with olive oil makes it so creamy and indulgent.

1. Preheat the oven to 400°F (200°C). Line a baking sheet with parchment paper.

2. Toss the broccoli florets and leeks with 1 tablespoon (15 mL) of the olive oil, 1 tablespoon (15 mL) of the grainy mustard, and the thyme leaves, salt, and pepper. After everything is coated, spread the mixture out on the lined baking sheet. Roast the vegetables until lightly browned and tender, about 15 to 18 minutes.

3. When they have slightly cooled, transfer the roasted vegetables to a food processor. Pulse the mixture until the broccoli is somewhat chopped. Set aside a spoonful of the chopped broccoli for garnish.

4. To the food processor, add the remaining ½ tablespoon (7 mL) of the grainy mustard and the lemon zest, lemon juice, salt, pepper, and nutritional yeast. Pulse until everything is combined. With the food processor running on low, drizzle in ⅓ cup (75 mL) of the olive oil through the feed tube. Continue to mix until you have a smooth, lightly chunky paste. Remove the bowl from the food processor, check the seasoning, and adjust if necessary.

5. Scrape the pâté mixture into a 2-cup (500 mL) nonreactive serving vessel, and scatter the reserved chopped broccoli over the top. Pour the remaining 1 tablespoon (15 mL) of the olive oil on top. Cover and place the pâté in the fridge for at least 2 hours or until the top oil layer has solidified a little bit.

6. Sprinkle the flaky sea salt over the pâté before you serve it with sliced bread, olives, pickles, and vegetables.

3 cups (750 mL) broccoli florets (from roughly 1 bunch of broccoli)

1 leek, white and light-green parts only, rough-chopped

⅓ cup + 2 tablespoons (75 mL + 30 mL) virgin olive oil, divided

1½ tablespoons (22 mL) grainy mustard, divided

2 teaspoons (10 mL) fresh thyme leaves (about 4 sprigs)

salt and pepper, to taste

2 teaspoons (10 mL) lemon zest

1½ tablespoons (22 mL) fresh lemon juice

2 tablespoons (30 mL) nutritional yeast

flaky sea salt, to taste

FOR SERVING

sliced bread (gluten free if required)

olives

pickles

vegetables

Homemade Popcorn *with* Magic Dust

SERVES *6 to 8*   FREE OF 🌿 🥣

The cashew-based dust really is magic on popcorn (and on plenty of other things). When you're blitzing the dust up in the food processor, be careful not to take it too far and make it into garlicky, cheesy cashew butter by accident. Although that wouldn't be so bad.

1. Place the raw cashews in the bowl of a food processor. Run the motor on high speed until the cashews have a mealy texture. To the ground cashews, add the nutritional yeast, arrowroot powder, sea salt, turmeric, garlic powder, and black pepper. Run the food processor on high again until you have an even, slightly coarse powder. This is your magic dust. Set aside.

2. Place a large bowl on your counter before you start popping the kernels.

3. In a large pot with a well-fitting lid (preferably a Dutch oven or something similar), heat the coconut oil and 3 popcorn kernels over medium-high heat. Cover.

4. Once the 3 kernels have popped, remove the lid and carefully remove the popped corn. Pour in the remaining popcorn kernels. Cover and remove the pot from the heat for 30 seconds.

5. Put the pot back on the heat and, with pot holders or kitchen towels in each hand, grab the handles of the pot and shake it with equal measures of vigor and control. I usually ball up a couple of thin kitchen towels in my hands and grab the handles while simultaneously holding the lid firmly down with my thumbs.

6. Shake the pot for roughly 2 minutes. The popcorn should be popping vigorously. Once the popping starts to slow, with about 3 seconds of silence between pops, remove the pot from the heat and take off the lid immediately.

7. As quickly and safely as you can, dump all the popcorn into the large bowl. Shake ¾ of the magic dust over top, and quickly mix it in with your hands. After the popcorn is evenly coated, garnish the top with the remaining magic dust and serve immediately.

⅓ cup (75 mL) raw cashews

2 tablespoons (30 mL) nutritional yeast

1 tablespoon (15 mL) arrowroot powder

2 teaspoons (10 mL) fine sea salt

½ teaspoon (2 mL) ground turmeric

½ teaspoon (2 mL) garlic powder

freshly ground black pepper, to taste

¼ cup (50 mL) refined coconut oil

⅔ cup (150 mL) organic popping corn

Sweet Potato Satays
with Peanut Lime Sauce

MAKES *16 to 20 skewers*   FREE OF 🌿 🥜   REQUIRES *time for prep*

I was making a stuffed sweet potato for dinner, as I often do
(see my Burrito-Stuffed Sweet Potatoes with Rustic Salsa on
page 169), and after drizzling some leftover peanut sauce on top,
I started thinking about those ubiquitous satay skewers that you
see at parties. I've grilled par-boiled sweet potatoes plenty of
times for salads because I love the smoky flavor that results, and I
knew that they would taste delicious with a peanut dipping sauce.
This recipe is the result of that thought process.

1. MAKE THE PEANUT LIME SAUCE: In a blender, combine the ginger, garlic,
    chili, peanut butter, lime juice, maple syrup, tamari, coconut milk, and
    grapeseed oil. Whiz the mixture on high until you have a smooth sauce,
    stopping to scrape down the sides if necessary. Set aside.

2. MAKE THE SWEET POTATO SATAYS: Cut the sweet potatoes into 5-inch
    (12.5 cm) sticks, roughly the size of standard steak fries. Place them in
    a large pot and cover them with water by about 1 inch (2.5 cm). Bring
    to a boil and simmer until the sweet potato sticks are just tender, about
    10 minutes.

3. Carefully drain the sweet potatoes. When they are cool enough to
    handle, thread the sweet potatoes onto the soaked wooden skewers,
    1 piece of sweet potato per skewer.

4. When you're finished skewering the sweet potatoes, lay them out on a
    platter or baking sheet. Brush the sweet potatoes with grapeseed oil on
    all sides, and season with salt and pepper.

5. Heat your grill to high. Place the sweet potatoes onto the grates and
    close the lid of the grill. Let the sweet potatoes cook about 3 minutes
    per side or until char marks appear.

6. Place the sweet potato satays on a serving platter alongside the Peanut
    Lime Sauce. Garnish the platter with the sliced green onions.

20 wooden skewers, soaked for at
least 30 minutes

PEANUT LIME SAUCE

1-inch (2.5 cm) piece of fresh
ginger, peeled

2 cloves garlic, peeled

1 small red chili pepper, seeded and
chopped

¼ cup (50 mL) natural peanut
butter

2 tablespoons (30 mL) fresh lime
juice

1 tablespoon (15 mL) pure maple
syrup

2 teaspoons (10 mL) gluten-free
tamari soy sauce

¼ cup (50 mL) full-fat coconut
milk OR water

2 tablespoons (30 mL) grapeseed
or other neutral-flavored oil,
plus extra for brushing the sweet
potatoes

SWEET POTATO SATAYS

2 medium sweet potatoes (about
2 pounds/1 kg)

salt and pepper, to taste

1 green onion, thinly sliced, for
garnish

Whipped Lentil Chipotle Dip

MAKES *about 2 cups (500 mL) of dip*   FREE OF 🌿 🍚
REQUIRES *time for prep*

This dip follows a similar preparation path to that of hummus, replacing the chickpeas with lentils, and the tahini with cashew butter. The result is an ultra-smooth, "whipped" texture with the smoky heat of chipotle peppers. I love spreading this onto toasted sourdough for a particularly good open-faced tomato sandwich.

1. Place the lentils in a medium saucepan and cover them with 3 cups (750 mL) of filtered water. Bring to a boil over medium-high heat. Lower to a simmer and cook until the lentils are mushy and falling apart, about 8 minutes.

2. While the lentils are cooking, combine the garlic, chipotles, adobo, if using, cashew butter, lemon juice, tomato paste, and cumin in a blender.

3. Drain the cooked lentils, and scrape them into the blender with the garlic and chipotle mixture. Season with salt and pepper. Whiz everything on high until the dip is completely smooth. You may have to stop the blender and scrape down the sides a couple of times.

4. The dip will be quite warm. For optimal serving, scrape the dip into a container and cover it with plastic wrap, pressing it onto the surface of the dip. Refrigerate the dip for at least 1 hour before serving.

5. You can garnish the top with a drizzle of olive oil, some extra ground cumin, and a sprinkle of paprika if you like.

1 cup (250 mL) split red lentils, rinsed

3 cloves garlic, peeled

2 chipotle peppers in adobo

1 tablespoon (15 mL) adobo sauce from the can (optional)

3 tablespoons (45 mL) raw cashew butter

1 tablespoon (15 mL) fresh lemon juice

1 teaspoon (5 mL) tomato paste

1½ teaspoons (7 mL) ground cumin

salt and pepper, to taste

GARNISHES (OPTIONAL)

virgin olive oil

ground cumin

sweet paprika

Gingered Brussels Sprout and
Shiitake Pot Stickers

MAKES *about 25 pot stickers*   FREE OF 🥄 🌰

These look fussy to make with their folded tops, but I assure you they're anything but. After I moisten the edge of the wonton wrapper, I quickly pinch and secure in any way I can to get the Brussels sprout and shiitake filling locked in. They wind up looking pretty in that "perfectly imperfect" way. If I'm serving these as a snack or an appetizer, I brown them ahead of time and just keep them warm on a low setting in the oven. The salty-sweet soy dip absolutely makes these.

1. MAKE THE DIPPING SAUCE: Whisk the tamari, maple syrup, ginger, green onion, and sesame seeds together in a small bowl. Set aside.

2. MAKE THE POT STICKERS: Heat the olive oil in a large sauté pan over medium heat. Add the shallots. Stir and cook until fragrant and translucent, about 3 minutes. Add the shiitake mushrooms. Stir and sauté the mushrooms until they start to soften, about 2 minutes. Add the Brussels sprouts, garlic, and ginger, and stir. Season everything with salt and pepper. Keep stirring the filling until the Brussels sprouts are bright green and slightly wilted, about 1 minute. Remove from the heat, and allow the filling to cool slightly.

3. Set out a small bowl of water. To assemble the pot stickers, divide the vegetable filling among the wonton wrappers, placing about 1 tablespoon (15 mL) of the filling in the center of each wonton wrapper. Take one filled wonton wrapper and dip your finger in the bowl of water. Moisten two sides of the wrapper, fold all sides together, and pinch along the edge to form a seal. Repeat with the remaining filled wrappers.

4. Wipe the sauté pan and heat a thin slick of olive oil over medium heat. Fry the pot stickers in batches until they're golden brown on all sides, about 1 full minute per side. Add more oil to the pan as needed to finish cooking all the pot stickers.

5. Serve the pot stickers hot with the dipping sauce on the side.

DIPPING SAUCE

¼ cup (50 mL) gluten-free tamari soy sauce

2 tablespoons (30 mL) pure maple syrup

½-inch (1 cm) piece of fresh ginger, peeled and finely grated with a Microplane grater

1 green onion, finely sliced

2 teaspoons (10 mL) sesame seeds

POT STICKERS

1 tablespoon (15 mL) virgin olive oil, plus extra for cooking

1 medium shallot, fine dice (about ¼ cup/50 mL diced shallot)

1 cup (250 mL) thinly sliced shiitake mushrooms

2 cups (500 mL) sliced Brussels sprouts (about ½ pound/227 g)

1 clove garlic, minced

1-inch (2.5 cm) piece of fresh ginger, peeled and minced

salt and pepper, to taste

25 wonton wrappers

Desserts & Small Treats

Most people enjoy a sweet ending, and I'd be lying if I told you that my early vegan cooking efforts weren't solely focused on re-creating all of my favorite dairy-laden desserts. Whenever I get a new cookbook, I always flip to this section first. So if you're like me, I'm happy to offer you a warm welcome to this book. All of these treats taste perfectly decadent and rich, but are all made with whole-grain or nut-based flours and natural sweeteners. I've included a few "Dessert Basics"—things like really good vegan ice cream and lemon curd—so that you can customize any recipe here in a new way. There are also some casual tea time–style treats as well. Every level of sweet tooth will be able to find something good here.

Stone Fruit Pecan Crumble

SERVES 6 FREE OF 🌿 💧 🌾

I love when a dessert can sensibly slide over to the breakfast category because of its virtuous ingredients, and this one is most certainly an example of that. I've served it as a "brunch dessert" with cultured coconut yogurt plenty of times. The crumble topping is just blitzed-up pecan halves with maple syrup and spice. It has all the crunch and buttery qualities of a traditional crumble topping though, without added oil or heaps of sugar. Feel free to customize this with whatever fruit, spices, or nuts you like. Once you have the ratios down and a good idea of how thick or thin to slice your fruit, you can make healthy crumble out of whatever you have on hand.

1. Preheat the oven to 375°F (190°C).

2. MAKE THE FILLING: In an 8-inch (20 cm) ovenproof dish, add the stone fruit, maple syrup, lemon juice, arrowroot powder, cinnamon, and sea salt, and lightly toss to combine. Set aside.

3. MAKE THE CRUMBLE TOPPING: In a food processor, combine the pecans, maple syrup, cinnamon, and sea salt. Pulse the mixture until you have a crumbly consistency.

4. Sprinkle the crumble mixture on top of the stone fruit. Bake the crumble until the fruit is tender and the topping has browned, 22 to 25 minutes. Serve warm or at room temperature.

FILLING

- 1¾ pounds (794 g) ripe stone fruit (plums, peaches, and nectarines are all great), pitted and sliced into ½-inch (1 cm) wedges (about 5 or 6 pieces of fruit)
- 2 tablespoons (30 mL) pure maple syrup
- 2 teaspoons (10 mL) fresh lemon juice
- 1 teaspoon (5 mL) arrowroot powder
- ½ teaspoon (2 mL) ground cinnamon
- ¼ teaspoon (1 mL) fine sea salt

CRUMBLE TOPPING

- 1¼ cups (300 mL) raw pecan halves
- 2 tablespoons (30 mL) pure maple syrup
- ¼ teaspoon (1 mL) ground cinnamon
- ¼ teaspoon (1 mL) fine sea salt

Pumpkin Mousse Parfaits

SERVES *4*   FREE OF 🌿 💧 🌾   REQUIRES *time for prep*

I used to love pumpkin pie and would eat it whenever it was available to me, but eventually, I started to get sick of it. Something about the dense, sometimes gummy, texture started putting me off. With most desserts, since we essentially bake the pumpkin twice, it can taste somewhat flat if it isn't treated right.

After enjoying a particularly delicious pumpkin spice smoothie made with coconut milk and banana, I started experimenting with ways to enjoy the vegetable in a lighter context. A mousse seemed like the perfect way to brighten the flavor and fluff up the texture. I use the cream from full-fat coconut milk as the base and just whip everything together in the food processor. It couldn't be simpler and the presentation is so pretty.

1. Remove the chilled can of coconut milk from the refrigerator. When you open the can, there should be a thick layer of pure coconut cream at the top. Scoop this coconut cream into the bowl of a food processor, being careful to avoid any of the water in the can. You should get about 1 cup (250 mL) of coconut cream. Reserve the coconut water for smoothies or discard.

2. To the coconut cream, add the pumpkin purée, maple syrup, lemon juice, arrowroot, vanilla, cinnamon, nutmeg, and sea salt. Whiz everything on high until you have a creamy and smooth mousse-like texture.

3. Portion the mousse into 4 serving vessels (I use water glasses), and top with the Whipped Coconut Cream and pecans. The mousse will keep in the refrigerator for up to 3 days.

1 can (13.5 ounces/400 mL) full-fat coconut milk, refrigerated overnight

¾ cup (175 mL) canned pure pumpkin purée

¼ cup (50 mL) pure maple syrup

½ teaspoon (2 mL) fresh lemon juice

1 tablespoon (15 mL) arrowroot powder

1 teaspoon (5 mL) pure vanilla extract

¾ teaspoon (3 mL) ground cinnamon

¼ teaspoon (1 mL) ground nutmeg

½ teaspoon (2 mL) fine sea salt

FOR SERVING

1 batch of Whipped Coconut Cream (page 271)

¼ cup (50 mL) pecan halves, toasted and chopped

Chocolate Chunk Ginger Cookies

MAKES *10 to 12 cookies*

I had my first taste of chocolate and ginger together in a rich cookie from a quaint café down the road from my parents' country home. It's a surprisingly craveable combination, and I turn to it constantly once the holidays roll around. These cookies have the perfect level of chewiness, and the little puddles of chocolate make them obsession-worthy. A gentle warning: these have a good amount of spice, so if you prefer your ginger cookies mellower and sweet, cut back the cinnamon, nutmeg, and ginger by half.

1. Preheat the oven to 350°F (180°C). Line a large baking sheet with parchment paper and set aside.

2. In a small bowl, whisk together the ground flaxseed and almond milk until frothy. Set aside for 5 minutes to thicken.

3. In a medium bowl, whisk together the spelt flour, baking soda, cinnamon, nutmeg, ginger, and sea salt. Set aside.

4. In the bowl of a stand mixer fitted with the paddle attachment, mix the coconut palm sugar, molasses, sunflower oil, and vanilla on high for 5 minutes. Stop the machine and add the ground flaxseed and almond milk mixture to the bowl. Mix for another full minute.

5. With the mixer on low, add the spelt flour mixture. Mix the dough for 2 minutes or until large clumps of flour are no longer visible.

6. Gently fold the chocolate chunks and crystalized ginger into the dough with a spatula until evenly distributed. The dough will be quite sticky.

7. Drop the dough in 1½-tablespoon (22 mL) pieces onto the prepared baking sheet, about 1½ inches (4 cm) apart. Lightly oil your hands and flatten the pieces of dough. Bake cookies for 12 minutes or until the undersides are just starting to brown and the tops feel dry to the touch. Cool cookies completely on the baking sheet.

½ tablespoon (7 mL) ground flaxseed

2 tablespoons (30 mL) unsweetened almond milk

1¼ cups (300 mL) whole spelt flour

½ teaspoon (2 mL) baking soda

1 teaspoon (5 mL) ground cinnamon

¼ teaspoon (1 mL) ground nutmeg

¼ teaspoon (1 mL) ground ginger

¼ teaspoon (1 mL) fine sea salt

½ cup (125 mL) coconut palm sugar

¼ cup + 1 tablespoon (50 mL + 15 mL) unsulfured molasses

2 tablespoons (30 mL) sunflower oil, plus extra

½ teaspoon (2 mL) pure vanilla extract

¼ cup (50 mL) vegan chocolate chunks

¼ cup (50 mL) chopped crystallized ginger OR more vegan chocolate chunks

Vanilla Corn Cake
with Roasted Strawberries

MAKES *one 9-inch (23 cm) cake* FREE OF 🥜 🌾

I had a corn-based cookie from a wildly popular bakery in New York one weekend, and on the way to the airport to fly home, I had to stop at that bakery and buy up a bunch of those golden cookies to take with me. That trip started my love affair with corn-based desserts. It made so much sense because I had always preferred cornbread with a noticeable sweet edge. I love the slightly crumbly texture that cornmeal brings to this cake. It tastes perfect with the jammy, roasted strawberries, but I imagine you could do this with plenty of other summer fruits.

¾ cup (175 mL) full-fat coconut milk

1 teaspoon (5 mL) fresh lemon juice

1 cup (250 mL) cornmeal (not coarse)

1 cup (250 mL) whole spelt flour

1 teaspoon (5 mL) lemon zest

1 tablespoon (15 mL) aluminum-free baking powder

¼ teaspoon (1 mL) baking soda

1 teaspoon (5 mL) fine sea salt

½ teaspoon (2 mL) ground turmeric (optional)

½ cup + 2 tablespoons (125 mL + 30 mL) pure maple syrup

½ cup (125 mL) sunflower oil, plus extra to grease pan

1 teaspoon (5 mL) vanilla bean paste OR pure vanilla extract

roughly 1 quart (4 cups/1 L) whole strawberries (smaller berries are preferable)

Whipped Coconut Cream (page 271), for serving (optional)

1. Preheat the oven to 350°F (180°C). Lightly grease a 9-inch (23 cm) round cake pan with sunflower oil. Cut a circle of parchment paper to fit in the bottom of the pan and press it in. Lightly grease the parchment, and set aside.

2. In a medium bowl, whisk together the coconut milk and lemon juice. Let this mixture sit for 5 minutes so that the milk can curdle slightly.

3. In a large bowl, whisk together the cornmeal, spelt flour, lemon zest, baking powder, baking soda, sea salt, and turmeric, if using.

4. Make a well in the center of the cornmeal mixture. Add the maple syrup, sunflower oil, vanilla, and coconut milk mixture. With a spatula, gently mix until you have a smooth and unified batter. Avoid overmixing.

5. Scrape the batter into the prepared cake pan and slide the pan into the oven. Bake the cake for 25 to 28 minutes or until the top is golden and a toothpick inserted into the center comes out clean. Let the cake cool completely. Raise the oven temperature to 400°F (200°C).

6. Cut the strawberries into halves or quarters (depending on size), and place them on a parchment-lined baking sheet. Slide the baking sheet into the oven and roast the strawberries until they become juicy and jammy, about 20 minutes.

7. Serve slices of the corn cake with a few roasted strawberries and some Whipped Coconut Cream if you like.

Fudgy Nut and Seed Butter Brownies

MAKES *16 brownies*   FREE OF 🌿 💧   REQUIRES *time for prep*

This may be my crowning achievement as far as desserts go, and I've tested it about a hundred times just to make sure. No added oil, no added refined sugar, no grains, loaded with chocolate, and they're vegan of course. These brownies are dense and fudgy, and taste great with a variety of nut or seed butters. I like to do a half almond/half hazelnut butter variation that mimics that popular chocolate hazelnut spread in flavor and richness.

1. Preheat the oven to 350°F (180°C). Line an 8-inch (2 L) square pan with a piece of parchment paper, leaving an overhang on two opposite sides. Set aside.

2. In a medium bowl, whisk together the nut or seed butter, maple syrup, applesauce, and vanilla.

3. To the nut butter mixture, add the cocoa powder, coconut flour, baking soda, and sea salt. Whisk to combine, ensuring that there are no dry lumps of cocoa in the batter.

4. In a double boiler, melt half of the chocolate chunks. Vigorously stir the melted chocolate into the brownie batter until fully incorporated.

5. Scrape the brownie batter into the prepared baking pan. Smooth the batter out evenly with a spatula, pushing it into the edges and corners of the pan.

6. Scatter the reserved chocolate chunks and rough-chopped nuts over the top. Slide the pan into the oven, and bake the brownies until the top is slightly firm and appears dry and lightly cracked, about 27 to 30 minutes.

7. Cool the brownies completely in the pan set on a wire rack. Then, cover the brownies and place them in the refrigerator for at least 1 hour. This step is crucial. The brownies will not cut neatly unless they get adequate cooling time.

8. I recommend running a chef's knife under hot water and drying it off right before slicing the brownies.

¾ cup (175 mL) smooth nut or seed butter (I like roasted almond, hazelnut, or sunflower butter)

¼ cup + 2 tablespoons (50 mL + 30 mL) pure maple syrup

¾ cup (175 mL) unsweetened applesauce

1½ teaspoons (7 mL) pure vanilla extract

½ cup (125 mL) unsweetened cocoa powder

3 tablespoons (45 mL) coconut flour

¾ teaspoon (3 mL) baking soda

½ teaspoon (2 mL) fine sea salt

½ cup (125 mL) vegan chocolate chunks OR chopped chocolate from a 70% dark, dairy-free chocolate bar, divided

3 tablespoons (45 mL) whole nuts OR seeds, rough-chopped (I like almonds, hazelnuts, or sunflower seeds)

No-Bake Salted Peanut Butter "Cookies"

MAKES *18 cookies*   FREE OF 🌾 🥣 💧   REQUIRES *time for prep*

While these treats aren't technically a cookie in the proper sense, they hit the spot when a sweet treat is needed to get through the afternoon. Fudgy Medjool dates form the bulk of the rich and sticky dough here. I find the lemon juice is necessary for adding dimension to the cookie. Otherwise, it's just sweetness piled on top of rich peanut butter, and your palate can't seem to catch a break. The flaky salt on top functions similarly to the lemon juice in that it takes this treat somewhere beyond pure sweetness.

If your dates are a bit dry, soak them in boiling water for 5 to 10 minutes. Drain the dates and proceed with the recipe.

1 cup (250 mL) raw almonds

½ cup (125 mL) unsalted smooth, natural peanut butter

1 cup (250 mL) Medjool dates, pitted

2 teaspoons (10 mL) pure vanilla extract

1 teaspoon (5 mL) fresh lemon juice

flaky sea salt, for sprinkling

1. Line a baking sheet with parchment paper and set aside.

2. In the bowl of a food processor, grind the raw almonds on high until you have a coarse meal, about 30 seconds.

3. Add the peanut butter, pitted dates, vanilla, and lemon juice to the food processor. Pulse the mixture a couple of times to get everything moving. Then mix with the food processor on high speed until you have a uniform "dough" that clumps together.

4. Using a rough measure of 1½ to 2 tablespoons (22 to 30 mL) per cookie, portion the dough into balls and place on the baking sheet. Press the balls down, either with the palm of your hand or the tines of a dinner fork. Sprinkle the tops of the cookies with the flaky sea salt.

5. Place the cookies in the refrigerator for at least an hour to firm up. The cookies can be stored in the refrigerator for up to 10 days.

Coconut Cream Tart

MAKES *a 9-inch (23 cm) tart*   FREE OF 🌿 🌾
REQUIRES *time for prep*

My mother says that this high-vibe version of coconut cream pie tastes like the "real thing" and brags about it to just about everyone, which I love. It benefits from having various forms of coconut (milk, oil, and shredded pieces) in all three components of the dessert. This is the dessert to bring out when you need to convince some vegan or health food skeptics of just how delicious, rich, and full the options are.

   Note that you have to chill one can of coconut milk overnight before making this recipe. The tart also has to set up in the fridge overnight.

1. Preheat the oven to 375°F (190°C). Lightly grease a 9-inch (23 cm) tart pan (at least 2 inches/5 cm deep) with coconut oil. Line the bottom of the pan with a circle of parchment paper, and set aside.

2. MAKE THE CRUST: In a food processor, grind the almonds until lightly chopped. Add the oats and coconut, and grind until everything is the texture of coarse sand. Add the sea salt, maple syrup, and 2 tablespoons (30 mL) of the almond milk, and mix until the crust dough starts to lump together. Use additional almond milk if necessary.

3. Press the crust mixture evenly into the prepared tart pan. Prick the crust with the tines of a fork, and then bake the crust until lightly golden, about 12 minutes. Let the crust cool completely on a wire rack.

4. MAKE THE FILLING: Rinse out the food processor bowl. Then add the coconut milk to the food processor, along with the shredded coconut, maple syrup, vanilla, sea salt, coconut oil, and arrowroot powder. Mix the filling on high until you have a smooth and even mixture with a little bit of texture from the coconut.

5. Pour the filling into the cooled crust. Place the tart in the refrigerator to set up overnight.

(recipe continues)

CRUST

½ cup (125 mL) raw almonds

1½ cups (375 mL) certified gluten-free rolled oats (not quick-cooking oats)

½ cup (125 mL) finely shredded unsweetened coconut

½ teaspoon (2 mL) fine sea salt

2 tablespoons (30 mL) pure maple syrup

2 to 3 tablespoons (30 to 45 mL) unsweetened almond milk OR water

FILLING

2 cups (500 mL) full-fat coconut milk

¾ cup (175 mL) finely shredded unsweetened coconut

⅓ cup (75 mL) pure maple syrup

2 teaspoons (10 mL) pure vanilla extract

¼ teaspoon (1 mL) fine sea salt

½ cup (125 mL) liquid virgin coconut oil, plus more to grease the tart pan

1½ teaspoons (7 mL) arrowroot powder

TOPPING

1 can (13.5 ounces/400 mL) full-fat coconut milk, chilled overnight

1 tablespoon (15 mL) pure maple syrup

½ teaspoon (2 mL) pure vanilla extract

unsweetened shredded coconut, toasted, for garnish (optional)

6.   MAKE THE TOPPING: Remove the chilled can of coconut milk from the refrigerator. When you open it, there should be a thick layer of pure coconut cream on top. Scoop this coconut cream into a medium bowl, being careful to avoid the water at the bottom of the can. Reserve the water for smoothies or discard. Add the maple syrup and vanilla to the bowl, and whisk by hand until you have a smooth and light cream.

7.   Spread the coconut cream topping onto the tart and garnish with toasted coconut if you like.

Raw Raspberry Cheesecake

MAKES *one 8-inch (20 cm) cake*   FREE OF 🌿 🌾
REQUIRES *time to soak and for prep*

I'm always excited to go out to a raw food restaurant for a full dinner. It reminds me of what is possible with whole foods treated lovingly, and it's usually just the kick I need when I'm in a recipe development rut. Dessert is undeniably my favorite part of the experience though.

My first brush with professional raw food finished with a strawberry cheesecake that I honestly did not shut up about for at least a week. How did they make it so rich? How did they make nuts taste like cream cheese? After some internet searching, I found out that raw cheesecakes could not be simpler to make, as long as you remember to soak the cashew base ahead of time. I serve slices of this on the small side because it is incredibly rich.

1. Using an 8-inch (20 cm) springform pan, release the ring so that the bottom disk comes away. Lay a piece of cling film over the bottom disk, covering its surface entirely. Secure the ring back onto the disk, aiming to get the cling film as taut as possible. Set aside.

2. MAKE THE CRUST: In a food processor, pulse the raw nuts or seeds, dates, coconut, vanilla, and sea salt. Keep pulsing until the nuts are finely chopped, and the crust mixture clumps together easily when you pinch it with your fingers. Press the crust into the prepared springform pan, forming an even layer across the bottom. Let the crust chill in the refrigerator while you make the filling.

3. MAKE THE FILLING: Drain and rinse the soaked cashews. Shake out any excess water. Place the drained cashews in either a high-speed blender or the rinsed bowl of your food processor. To the cashews, add the lemon juice, maple syrup, coconut oil, almond milk, kombucha, vanilla, nutritional yeast, and sea salt. Mix the filling on the highest speed until you have a totally smooth and thick cream-like texture, about 4 to 5 minutes.

(recipe continues)

CRUST

2 cups (500 mL) raw nuts OR seeds of your choice (I like almonds, pecans, and sunflower seeds)

1 cup (250 mL) Medjool dates, pitted

¼ cup (50 mL) unsweetened finely shredded coconut

½ teaspoon (2 mL) pure vanilla extract

¼ teaspoon (1 mL) fine sea salt

FILLING

2½ cups (625 mL) raw cashews, soaked for at least 6 hours

¼ cup (50 mL) fresh lemon juice

½ cup (125 mL) pure maple syrup

½ cup (125 mL) liquid refined coconut oil

¼ cup (50 mL) unsweetened almond milk

¼ cup (50 mL) plain or unflavored kombucha OR more almond milk

1 tablespoon (15 mL) pure vanilla extract

½ teaspoon (2 mL) nutritional yeast

½ teaspoon (2 mL) fine sea salt

TOPPING

1 pint (1½ cups/375 mL) fresh raspberries, divided

1 tablespoon (15 mL) pure maple syrup

½ teaspoon (2 mL) fresh lemon juice

4. Scrape the filling into the springform pan and spread it out evenly over the pressed-in crust. Place the cake in the refrigerator and let it firm up overnight.

5. RIGHT BEFORE SERVING, MAKE THE TOPPING: In a small bowl, mash ½ cup (125 mL) of the raspberries with the maple syrup and lemon juice. It should have a thin, slightly jammy consistency. Spread this sauce evenly over the surface of the cheesecake. Garnish the top with the remaining fresh raspberries and serve right away. This cake slices best right out of the refrigerator.

Banana Bread Scones

MAKES *8 to 10 scones*   FREE OF 🥥

These scones are surprisingly tender considering that they're made entirely out of whole-grain flour. The banana and buttery coconut oil keep them moist and lightly sweet. I've tried vegan scone recipes with cold coconut oil cut into the dry ingredients (like butter is with traditional scone recipes), but I honestly like these better, and they're much easier to make. Replacing the walnuts or dates with chopped vegan chocolate is always a good idea.

2 cups (500 mL) whole spelt flour

1 tablespoon (15 mL) aluminum-free baking powder

1 teaspoon (5 mL) ground cinnamon

½ teaspoon (2 mL) fine sea salt

⅓ cup (75 mL) pure maple syrup

⅓ cup (75 mL) liquid refined coconut oil, plus extra for greasing the measuring cup

2 teaspoons (10 mL) pure vanilla extract

½ cup (125 mL) mashed ripe banana (about 1 large banana)

2 tablespoons (30 mL) hot water

⅓ cup (75 mL) chopped walnuts

⅓ cup (75 mL) Medjool dates, pitted and chopped

FOR SERVING

coconut butter

jam

1. Preheat the oven to 350°F (180°C). Line a baking sheet with parchment paper, and set aside.

2. In a large bowl, whisk together the spelt flour, baking powder, cinnamon, and sea salt. Make a small well in the center of the flour mixture and add the maple syrup, coconut oil, vanilla, and mashed banana to the bowl. Gently stir the mixture with a spatula until the ingredients are slightly combined but there are still jags of flour throughout.

3. Add the hot water, chopped walnuts, and dates to the bowl and stir until everything is evenly combined. Avoid overmixing.

4. Lightly grease a ⅓-cup (75 mL) measuring cup with coconut oil. Scoop the scone batter up with the measuring cup and drop onto the prepared baking sheet with a little force. The portion of scone dough should come out in a nice puck shape. Repeat with remaining dough, spacing each scone 2 inches (5 cm) apart, and re-greasing the measuring cup if necessary.

5. Bake the scones for 20 minutes. Allow them to cool slightly on a wire rack before enjoying with coconut butter and jam.

Blueberry Muffin Loaf

MAKES *1 loaf* FREE OF 🥜

This loaf has all the comfort of a typical crumb-topped blueberry muffin but supersized into one cozy loaf. It's lightly sweet with a nice warm hit of vanilla, cinnamon, and orange. Spelt flour is essentially my all-purpose flour at home, but it seems to truly shine in recipes like this. Its natural, nutty sweetness is perfect with simple cakes that feature fruit and spice.

I know maple sugar can be quite expensive in some areas, so it's good to know that coconut palm sugar can be substituted for the maple sugar with virtually no change in the taste or texture of the loaf. Frozen blueberries right out of the freezer (always in season) work beautifully for this recipe as well.

1. Preheat the oven to 375°F (190°C). Lightly grease an 8- × 4-inch (1.5 L) loaf pan with sunflower oil. Line the pan with parchment paper, leaving an overhang on the two long sides, and set aside.

2. MAKE THE CRUMBLE TOPPING: In a small bowl, combine maple sugar, spelt flour, sea salt, cinnamon, and sunflower oil. Lightly mix the topping with a fork until it starts clumping. Place the topping in the refrigerator while you make the loaf.

3. MAKE THE LOAF: In a measuring cup, lightly whisk the almond milk with the orange juice, and set aside to curdle.

4. In a large bowl, whisk together the spelt flour, almond flour, baking powder, baking soda, sea salt, and cinnamon. Add the almond milk mixture to the flour mixture. Add the applesauce, sunflower oil, maple sugar, and vanilla. Gently mix with a spatula until you have a unified batter, being careful not to overmix.

5. Gently fold the blueberries into the batter. Quickly scrape the batter into the prepared loaf pan, and top it with the crumble mixture. Gently press the crumble mixture into the surface of the loaf with your fingers. The crumble pieces should be surrounded by batter without being submerged. Slide the loaf pan into the oven, and bake for 55 to 60 minutes or until evenly browned on the top and a toothpick inserted into the center of the loaf comes out clean.

6. Cool the loaf completely in the pan before slicing and serving.

TOPPING

¼ cup (50 mL) maple sugar OR coconut palm sugar

4 tablespoons (60 mL) whole spelt flour

small pinch of fine sea salt

¼ teaspoon (1 mL) ground cinnamon

2 tablespoons (30 mL) sunflower or other neutral-flavored oil

LOAF

⅓ cup (75 mL) unsweetened almond milk

1 tablespoon (15 mL) fresh orange juice

1½ cups (375 mL) whole spelt flour

½ cup (125 mL) almond flour

2 teaspoons (10 mL) aluminum-free baking powder

¼ teaspoon (1 mL) baking soda

½ teaspoon (2 mL) fine sea salt

1 teaspoon (5 mL) ground cinnamon

¼ cup (50 mL) unsweetened applesauce

⅓ cup (75 mL) sunflower or other neutral-flavored oil, plus extra for greasing the pan

⅓ cup + 2 tablespoons (75 mL + 30 mL) maple sugar

1 teaspoon (5 mL) pure vanilla extract

1 cup (250 mL) fresh blueberries OR frozen blueberries

Chocolate Macaroon Cookie Truffles

MAKES *18 large truffles*   FREE OF 🌿   REQUIRES *time for prep*

I make huge batches of these around the holidays to bundle up as healthy, but indulgent, gifts. The mix of coconut butter (a product that contains coconut flesh and oil), vanilla, and almond flour makes for a convincing raw cookie dough sensation. Whether or not they admit it, almost everyone loves raw cookie dough. This is the safest (no raw eggs!), most elegant, and delicious way to eat it that I've come up with so far.

1. In the bowl of a food processor, combine the oat flour, almond flour, shredded coconut, sea salt, soft coconut butter, 1 tablespoon (15 mL) of the coconut oil, the maple syrup, and vanilla. Mix on high until you have a cookie-dough-like consistency.

2. Line a baking sheet or dinner plate with parchment paper. Scoop 1 tablespoon (15 mL) of the dough per truffle, and gently roll into a ball before placing on the parchment-lined surface. Repeat with the remaining dough. Transfer the truffles to the refrigerator for at least 30 minutes.

3. In a double boiler, melt the chocolate chips with the remaining teaspoon of coconut oil. Once the chocolate is liquefied, carefully remove it from the heat.

4. Using a fork or small slotted spoon, lower a truffle into the melted chocolate and lightly toss it around to coat. Carefully lift the truffle out and lay it back onto the parchment. Garnish the top with some shredded coconut. Repeat with remaining truffles. Place the truffles back in the refrigerator to firm up.

5. The truffles will keep in a sealed container in the refrigerator for about 1 week.

1¼ cups (300 mL) certified gluten-free oat flour

½ cup (125 mL) almond flour

½ cup (125 mL) unsweetened finely shredded coconut, plus extra for garnish

¼ teaspoon (1 mL) fine sea salt

4 tablespoons (60 mL) soft coconut butter

1 tablespoon + 1 teaspoon (15 mL + 5 mL) liquid virgin coconut oil, divided

¼ cup + 1 tablespoon (50 mL + 15 mL) pure maple syrup

½ teaspoon (2 mL) pure vanilla extract

1 cup (250 mL) vegan semi-sweet chocolate chips

Salted Chocolate Truffles

MAKES *18 truffles*   FREE OF 🌿 🥜 💧   REQUIRES *time for prep*

I could eat just one of these for dessert and be satisfied. They're so rich, and the extra sprinkle of salt intensifies the chocolate flavor big time. The high fat content of the coconut milk helps this truffle mixture firm up just like a typical dairy-based one. A splash of liqueur or whiskey in these is arguably necessary around holiday time.

12 ounces (360 g) vegan dark chocolate

⅔ cup (150 mL) full-fat coconut milk

1 teaspoon (5 mL) fine sea salt

½ cup (125 mL) unsweetened cocoa powder

1. Set up a double boiler with a medium saucepan and medium, nonreactive bowl. Break up the chocolate into pieces, and transfer them to the bowl along with the coconut milk and sea salt.

2. Place the bowl over the simmering water. Let it sit for about a minute. Then, start stirring occasionally with a spatula. Once you have a melted, smooth mixture, remove the bowl from the heat. Let the truffle mixture cool to room temperature, and then place it in the refrigerator for at least 6 hours, preferably overnight.

3. Line a small baking sheet with parchment paper.

4. Once the truffle mixture is set and fully chilled, scoop out full tablespoons onto the parchment-lined sheet. Once you've scooped out all the truffles, transfer the baking sheet to the refrigerator for 30 minutes.

5. Place the cocoa powder in a shallow bowl.

6. Remove the scooped truffle mixture from the refrigerator. Working quickly, roll the portioned mixture into balls. Then, roll those balls in the cocoa powder. Try to gently shake off any excess cocoa powder, and then place the truffles back on the baking sheet.

7. The truffles will keep in a sealed container in the refrigerator for about 1 week.

Hippie Bonbons

MAKES *19 bonbons*   FREE OF 🌿 💧 🥥

This is a typical date and nut energy ball sort of mix with the volume turned up. Orange zest and cinnamon perk these treats up tremendously and help to make them special, too. I make them truffle sized, but you could go bigger if you want to fashion these into a healthy snack cookie or bar on the go. They're great, portable fuel for long hikes.

1. In the bowl of a food processor, combine the pitted dates, nuts or seeds, orange juice, orange zest, vanilla, sea salt, and cinnamon. Pulse the mixture a couple of times to chop everything. Then mix on high speed until the mixture sticks together and the nut pieces are quite small.

2. Scoop out a heaped tablespoon portion of the date and nut mixture, and roll the portion into a ball. Set the bonbon onto a dinner plate. Repeat with the remaining date and nut mixture.

3. The bonbons will keep in a sealed container in the refrigerator for about 1 week.

1½ cups (375 mL) Medjool dates, pitted

1 cup (250 mL) mixed raw nuts OR seeds (I like almonds, pecans, and sunflower seeds)

1 tablespoon (15 mL) fresh orange juice

½ teaspoon (2 mL) orange zest

1 teaspoon (5 mL) pure vanilla extract

½ teaspoon (2 mL) fine sea salt

½ teaspoon (2 mL) ground cinnamon

Beet Velvet Slice
with Tangy Citrus Frosting

MAKES *1 loaf cake* FREE OF 🌿 🥜 REQUIRES *time to soak and for prep*

This "cake" doesn't go near an oven, but the texture is still remarkably similar to a dense cake or bar. I did an internship at a raw food restaurant and learned that the secret behind their mind-boggling raw cakes is a combination of almond or nut meal, soft Medjool dates, and melted coconut oil. The nuts and dates make for a spongy texture, and the coconut oil holds everything together after the dessert is refrigerated. Making impossibly rich desserts out of fruit, nuts, oils, and extracts was nothing short of a revelation to me at the time. It was inspiring but also wonderful to know that I could start eating my dessert creations for breakfast.

1. Line an 8- × 4-inch (1.5 L) loaf pan with parchment paper, leaving an overhang on the two long sides. Set aside.

2. MAKE THE CAKE: In the bowl of a food processor, pulse the pitted dates with the filtered water until a chunky paste begins to form. Scrape the date paste into a large bowl. To the date paste, add the almond flour, coconut oil, vanilla, cacao powder, sea salt, and grated beets. Mix the batter with a spatula or your hands until everything is evenly mixed.

3. Press the cake mixture into the parchment-lined loaf pan until it is evenly thick and you've filled out the pan to the corners. Cover the cake with plastic wrap, and set in the fridge until you're ready to frost it.

4. MAKE THE FROSTING: In a blender or food processor, combine the drained macadamia nuts, almond milk, maple syrup, lemon juice, vanilla, and salt. Blend this mixture on high until it is a smooth and creamy consistency. Reduce the speed to low, remove the top of the blender, and slowly pour in the melted coconut oil. Once you have a homogeneous mixture, turn off the machine.

5. Scrape the frosting into a bowl. Cover the frosting with plastic wrap, pressing it onto the surface. Allow the frosting to firm up in the refrigerator for about 1 hour.

6. Spread the frosting evenly over the surface of the cake. Cover the frosted cake with plastic wrap, and let it set up in the refrigerator for at least 30 minutes. When ready to serve, lift the cake by pulling up on the overhanging parchment paper. Slice and serve with a sprinkle of cacao powder if you like.

CAKE

1 cup (250 mL) Medjool dates, pitted

1 to 2 tablespoons (15 to 30 mL) filtered water

2 cups (500 mL) almond flour

¼ cup (50 mL) liquid refined coconut oil

1 tablespoon (15 mL) pure vanilla extract

2 tablespoons (30 mL) raw cacao powder, plus some extra for garnish

pinch of fine sea salt

1 cup (250 mL) finely grated red beets (about 2 medium, peeled beets), squeezed in an old kitchen towel to remove excess moisture

FROSTING

1 cup (250 mL) raw macadamia nuts, soaked for at least 6 hours and drained

⅓ cup (75 mL) almond milk

¼ cup (50 mL) pure maple syrup

3 tablespoons (45 mL) fresh lemon juice

1½ teaspoons (7 mL) pure vanilla extract

pinch of fine sea salt

⅓ cup (75 mL) melted refined coconut oil

Chocolate Cupcakes Deluxe

MAKES *12 cupcakes*   FREE OF 🥜   REQUIRES *time for prep*

I only bake with whole-grain flours or nut or seed flours, which can be particularly challenging when trying to come up with a tender, special occasion cake that doesn't eat like a bran muffin. This is where almond flour comes in handy. It helps whole-grain cakes win back that moist and tender texture. It's especially delicious in this chocolate cake batter because almond naturally enhances the flavor of chocolate. This is the only cupcake recipe that I make, always with the Whipped Coconut Cream (page 271) for frosting. Sometimes I finish them off with shredded coconut, chopped nuts, or fresh berries. A drizzle of Maple Caramel (page 274) is the ultimate though.

It's best to make the Whipped Coconut Cream and Maple Caramel the day before you bake the cupcakes. Once the cakes cool, you can just grab them and finish everything off in no time.

1. Preheat the oven to 350°F (180°C). Place cupcake liners in a 12-cup muffin pan, or grease them with extra coconut oil. Set aside.

2. In a large bowl, whisk together the spelt flour, almond flour, cocoa powder, baking powder, baking soda, and sea salt. Squeeze out any almond flour lumps.

3. Combine the almond milk and apple cider vinegar in a bowl, and set aside for 2 minutes.

4. To the flour mixture, add the maple syrup, coconut oil, vanilla, and hot coffee. Add the almond milk mixture. Gently stir the batter with a spatula until all flour is absorbed, being careful not to overmix.

5. Quickly portion the batter into the muffin cups and slide the muffin pan into the oven. Bake the cupcakes until a toothpick inserted in the center of one emerges clean, about 20 to 23 minutes. Let the cupcakes cool completely.

6. Spread the Whipped Coconut Cream on top of the cooled cupcakes and drizzle with the Maple Caramel. Serve immediately.

7. If you want to make these ahead of time, I would recommend applying the Whipped Coconut Cream and Maple Caramel to the cupcakes just before serving. The cupcakes themselves can be made up to 2 days in advance if wrapped tightly.

1¼ cups (300 mL) whole spelt flour

½ cup (125 mL) almond flour

¾ cup (175 mL) unsweetened cocoa powder

1 teaspoon (5 mL) aluminum-free baking powder

1 teaspoon (5 mL) baking soda

¼ teaspoon (2 mL) fine sea salt

1 cup (250 mL) unsweetened almond milk

1 teaspoon (5 mL) apple cider vinegar

¾ cup (175 mL) pure maple syrup

⅓ cup (75 mL) liquid coconut oil

1 teaspoon (5 mL) pure vanilla extract

½ cup (125 mL) hot brewed coffee

1 batch Whipped Coconut Cream (page 271)

½ batch Maple Caramel (page 274)

Earl Grey Tiramisu

SERVES *8 to 10*   FREE OF 🌾 🥜   REQUIRES *time to soak and for prep*

My grandmother's family came to Canada from Italy when she was a kid, and she was an excellent cook of many Italian specialties. Despite expressing her interest in the dessert, she would never touch even a single bite of tiramisu because she was afraid of consuming raw eggs. I think she would have loved this version because, first, it has no eggs. Second, it has the gentle citrus flavor of Earl Grey tea with tons of warm and fragrant vanilla. It kind of reminds me of an Earl Grey latte in dessert form.

The cookies are made entirely out of almond meal. I store my almond meal in the refrigerator for a longer shelf life, but when I make these cookies, I take it out and let it sit at room temperature the day before. It seems to perform in a more predictable way when at room temperature.

1. Preheat the oven to 350°F (180°C). Line a baking sheet with parchment paper, and set aside.

2. MAKE THE COOKIES: With a fork, mix the almond flour, Earl Grey tea, lemon zest, maple syrup, coconut oil, and vanilla together in a medium bowl, breaking up the chunks of coconut oil as you go.

3. Bring the cookie dough together with your hands, and transfer it to the parchment-lined baking sheet. Press and form the dough into a narrow oval-like shape. Start flattening the dough out with your hands. If your dough is a bit sticky, lay a sheet of plastic wrap over the surface, and roll it out with a rolling pin. You're aiming for a piece of dough that's roughly 10 × 7 inches (25 × 18 cm) and ¼ inch (5 mm) thick.

4. Slide the baking sheet into the oven and bake for 12 minutes or until the edges have the faintest hint of brown.

5. Remove the large cookie from the oven. Carefully cut the large cookie into 1-inch (2.5 cm) strips along the short side. Separate the cookies as much as you can with your knife. You should have about 10 to 12 cookies total. Some cookies will be much longer than others, but we'll address this in step 9.

(recipe continues)

COOKIES

1½ cups (375 mL) almond flour

2 teaspoons (10 mL) loose-leaf Earl Grey tea, ground into a powder

1 teaspoon (5 mL) lemon zest

¼ cup (50 mL) pure maple syrup

2 tablespoons (30 mL) refined coconut oil, solid

½ teaspoon (2 mL) pure vanilla extract

CASHEW MASCARPONE FILLING

2½ cups (625 mL) raw cashews, soaked for at least 6 hours and drained

1¼ cups (300 mL) strong-brewed Earl Grey tea, divided

½ cup (125 mL) fresh lemon juice

½ cup (125 mL) pure maple syrup

1 tablespoon (15 mL) pure vanilla extract

½ teaspoon (2 mL) fine sea salt

⅛ teaspoon (0.5 mL) nutritional yeast

⅓ cup (75 mL) liquid refined coconut oil

cocoa powder OR shavings from a vegan dark chocolate bar, for serving

6. Slide the baking sheet back into the oven. Bake the cookies 8 to 10 minutes more or until evenly golden brown on the sides. Allow the cookies to cool completely.

7. MAKE THE CASHEW MASCARPONE FILLING: Rinse and drain the cashews and place them in a blender. To the blender, add ¼ cup (50 mL) of the Earl Grey tea, the lemon juice, maple syrup, vanilla, salt, and nutritional yeast. Blend the mixture on high, stopping to scrape the sides down a couple of times. Blend until the mixture has just a few tiny lumps.

8. With the blender on low, open the small feed hole, and drizzle in the coconut oil. Stop the blender and replace the feed hole lid. Blend the mixture on high one more time until completely smooth.

9. Pour the remaining 1 cup (250 mL) of the Earl Grey tea into a shallow dish with a lip. Place an 8- × 10-inch (20 × 25 cm) serving dish alongside. Take your cooled cookies and break any of the longer ones so that all are roughly the same size.

10. Dip the cookies, one at a time, into the Earl Grey tea. Quickly turn the cookies to coat before placing in the serving dish. Once you've soaked and arranged all of the cookies in the dish, pour the cashew mascarpone mixture over top. Smooth it out over the cookies in an even layer.

11. Place the tiramisu in the refrigerator to set up for 8 hours or overnight. Serve the tiramisu with a dusting of cocoa powder or chocolate shavings on top.

Decadent No-Dairy Ice Cream

MAKES *about 4 cups (1 L)* FREE OF 🌿 🥥
REQUIRES *time to soak and for prep*

I serve ice cream with Chocolate Magic Shell (page 270), Maple Caramel (page 274), and a bunch of chopped fruit, nuts, coconut, and other toppings as a dinner party dessert all the time. Guests get to have exactly what they like, and the childhood birthday party nostalgia puts a smile on everyone's face. I came up with this recipe after my ice cream maker seemed to stop working. I often make a banana "soft serve" by blitzing slices of frozen banana in my food processor, so I thought I could employ a similar strategy with a cashew-and-coconut-based ice cream.

And it really works! I make the ice cream base, freeze it in ice cube molds, and then "churn" the frozen cubes into ice cream with a bit of water. From there, you can enjoy it as a decadent soft serve or you can scrape it into a container for a hard freeze. Delicious either way!

1. Drain the cashews and place them in a blender along with the coconut milk. Blend on high until you have a smooth, very thick cream. You may have to stop the blender and scrape down the sides a couple of times before it gets to this stage.

2. Pour the cashew and coconut cream mixture into a medium saucepan. Add the chopped cacao butter and maple syrup. Put the saucepan over medium-low heat, and whisk frequently until all of the cacao has melted.

3. Remove the cashew coconut mixture from the heat, and whisk in the vanilla, arrowroot powder, lemon juice, and sea salt until fully combined.

4. Carefully pour the mixture into clean ice cube molds. Slide the ice cube molds into the freezer, and let them rest until almost totally solid, about 6 hours.

5. Remove the ice cube molds from the freezer, and empty the cubes out into the food processor. Add the filtered water. Pulse the mixture a few times to break up the chunks. Then, whiz it on high until it has a creamy and thick mixture. It should appear similar to soft serve ice cream.

(recipe continues)

BASIC VANILLA

1½ cups (375 mL) raw cashews, soaked for at least 6 hours

1 can (13.5 ounces/400 mL) full-fat coconut milk

1 ounce (28 g) cacao butter, chopped

½ cup (125 mL) pure maple syrup

1 tablespoon (15 mL) pure vanilla extract

1 teaspoon (5 mL) arrowroot powder

1 teaspoon (5 mL) fresh lemon juice

½ teaspoon (2 mL) fine sea salt

½ cup (125 mL) filtered water

CHOCOLATE

To the Basic Vanilla recipe add

⅓ cup (75 mL) vegan chocolate chips, melted

3 tablespoons (45 mL) unsweetened cocoa powder

STRAWBERRY (*or other fruit of your choice*)

To the Basic Vanilla recipe add

1⅓ cups (325 mL) chopped strawberries

1 tablespoon (15 mL) pure maple syrup

1 teaspoon (5 mL) fresh lemon juice

6. Taste the ice cream for sweetness at this point since freezing tends to alter sweet flavors. Add more maple syrup if you like at this stage.

7. Enjoy immediately or scrape the ice cream into a container and store it in the freezer. If you put the ice cream in for a hard freeze, it should be allowed to soften at room temperature for about 20 minutes before serving.

FOR THE CHOCOLATE VARIATION: Proceed with the recipe as written, but at the saucepan stage, when you melt the cacao butter into the ice cream base (step 2), throw the chocolate chips and cocoa powder in as well.

FOR THE STRAWBERRY VARIATION: Before beginning the recipe, in a small bowl stir together the chopped strawberries, maple syrup, and lemon juice. Let the mixture sit while you prepare the ice cream base. It will get a little bit juicy. Stir the mixture with all its liquid into the ice cream base when you remove it from the heat (step 3). Proceed with the basic recipe.

Chocolate Magic Shell

MAKES *½ cup (125 mL)*   FREE OF 🌿 🥜 🥥

This chocolate shell can fix any less-than-perfect-looking dessert. It's easy to throw together and nice to have on hand along with some Decadent No-Dairy Ice Cream (page 267). When poured over very cold ice cream, the coconut oil in the sauce firms the mixture up, making a perfect chocolate casing to crack through.

3 tablespoons (45 mL) liquid coconut oil

¼ cup (50 mL) pure maple syrup

¼ cup (50 mL) unsweetened cocoa powder, sifted

½ teaspoon (2 mL) pure vanilla extract

⅛ teaspoon (0.5 mL) fine sea salt

1. In a medium bowl, whisk the coconut oil, maple syrup, cocoa powder, vanilla, and sea salt together until you have a smooth sauce. Store covered at room temperature for up to 5 days.

2. If your room's temperature tends to be cool, the coconut oil may solidify the sauce. If I have the sauce in a glass jar, I usually just run it under hot running tap water until it fully liquefies. You could also warm it up over low heat in a small saucepan if you like.

Whipped Coconut Cream

MAKES *a generous 1 cup (250 mL)*   FREE OF 🌿 🥜 💧 🌾 REQUIRES *time for prep*

Simply delicious on almost any dessert. Whipping coconut milk solids into cream is a fundamental skill in the world of vegan sweets. Certain brands of coconut milk tend to firm up better than others. Grocery stores are kept at cooler temperatures, so you can get a feel for how much solid cream you'll be able to retrieve from a can by lightly shaking it at the store before you buy it. If you hear a lot of sloshing, move on to the next one. The can should feel like a solid mass, with little inner movement when you shake it.

1 can (13.5 ounces/400 mL) full-fat coconut milk, chilled overnight

1 tablespoon (15 mL) pure maple syrup

½ teaspoon (2 mL) pure vanilla extract

1. Remove the chilled can of coconut milk from the refrigerator. When you open it, there should be a thick layer of pure coconut cream on top. Scoop this coconut cream into a medium bowl, being careful to avoid the water at the bottom of the can. Reserve the water for smoothies or discard.

2. To the coconut cream, add the maple syrup and vanilla and whisk vigorously by hand until you have a smooth and light cream. You could also whip this in a blender, food processor, or with a hand mixer.

Dreamy Lemon Curd

MAKES *a generous 1 cup (250 mL)*   FREE OF 🌿 🥜 🌾

I know this is the dessert chapter, but I mostly make this lemon curd for my breakfast toast and porridge bowls in the morning. I keep it just a little bit tart for this reason. The thickener here is arrowroot powder and it works beautifully. You could use any citrus juice you like—blood orange juice, grapefruit juice, and lime juice all make great curds. I would leave the ground turmeric out of the recipe if you're using any citrus other than lemon though, since I use it mostly for that bright yellow color. This curd is particularly nice dolloped on top of the Vanilla Corn Cake (page 240).

¼ cup (50 mL) maple syrup OR raw agave nectar

½ cup (125 mL) full-fat coconut milk

⅓ cup (75 mL) fresh lemon juice

¼ cup (50 mL) room temperature coconut oil

⅛ teaspoon (0.5 mL) ground turmeric

⅛ teaspoon (0.5 mL) sea salt

2 teaspoons (10 mL) lemon zest

2 tablespoons (30 mL) arrowroot powder

1. In a medium saucepan over medium heat, combine the maple syrup, coconut milk, lemon juice, coconut oil, ground tumeric, sea salt, and lemon zest. Bring the mixture to a light boil, whisking occasionally.

2. When some bubbles start to break the surface, add the arrowroot powder to the saucepan, and whisk constantly as the mixture simmers. After the curd has thickened enough to coat the back of a spoon rather thickly, remove from the heat.

3. Quickly scrape the curd into a jar or bowl. Let it cool slightly at room temperature before pressing a piece of plastic wrap onto the surface of the curd. Store the lemon curd in the refrigerator for up to 1 week.

Maple Caramel

MAKES *almost 1¼ cups (300 mL)*   FREE OF 🌿 🥜 💧 🌾
REQUIRES *time for prep*

I saw a video on a food media website where they were making a cheat's caramel of sorts by combining brown sugar and cream in a saucepan, and simmering it down until it reached a thick, saucy texture. I immediately had to try it with maple syrup and coconut milk as an experiment. Within 45 minutes, I was happily dipping apple slices in my cane sugar–free caramel creation. The lemon juice gives the sauce some character and dimension that I find necessary given the richness of coconut milk and maple syrup.

1 cup (250 mL) full-fat coconut milk

¾ cup (175 mL) pure maple syrup

1 teaspoon (5 mL) pure vanilla extract

1 teaspoon (5 mL) fresh lemon juice

¾ teaspoon (3 mL) fine sea salt

1. Combine the coconut milk and maple syrup in a medium saucepan over medium-high heat. Once the mixture comes to a boil, lower the heat to a strong simmer.

2. The caramel will be bubbling continuously. Whisk it every couple of minutes. Keep simmering and whisking the caramel for about 15 minutes or until the volume of the liquid has reduced by ⅓. It will have thickened slightly.

3. Stir the vanilla, lemon juice, and sea salt into the caramel while it's still warm. Scrape the caramel into a bowl or glass jar. Let the caramel come to room temperature before covering and storing in the refrigerator. Caramel is at ideal texture after refrigerating overnight and will keep for 1 week.

Thank you!

This book started as a tiny seedling in the back of my mind. It changed and grew slowly over time, with the care of so many dedicated and talented people. Your reassurance has brought this project into full bloom, and my gratitude will never be enough.

Mark, your jokes and hugs gave me fierce determination when the repeated recipe testing and marathon photo days got to be a little much. Thank you for always running out to get me the prettiest lettuces, for making me tea when I needed to re-center, for eating literally every test round from this book, and for matching my drive and tenacity with calm encouragement, always. You have the biggest piece of my heart.

My family—Mom, Dad, and Tom: thank you for your unwavering support, and for all of your real-talk moments throughout this project as well. Mom, you are the most selfless and determined person I know. Thank you for helping me find that fire and drive to succeed, no matter what. Dad, beginning when I was very young, you taught me that working harder and smarter would take me everywhere I needed to be. Tom, thanks for always scrounging up my last-minute grocery requests, and for always finding a way to make me chuckle.

To my amazing friend Michelle, would this book have even happened if we hadn't crossed paths? Doubtful. Thanks for your gentle persistence and your constant encouragement. I have a career and a life that I love, and I owe a lot of that to you.

To my incredible editor Andrea Magyar, thank you for believing in this project, for guiding me through the process with reassurance, and for supporting my vision through it all. Thank you to Lucia Watson as well, and everyone from the Penguin/Avery team. I still can't believe that this whole thing is real because it's been such a dream to work together.

To my literary agent Sharon Bowers, thank you for all those gentle nudges that made this book come to life. Your humor and guidance meant everything when I was trying to wrap my head around this whole process and keep the insecurities at bay.

My recipe testers: thank you for your honest feedback, for your infectious excitement, for sending all those photographs, for making suggestions, and for your glowing encouragement.

Lastly and most importantly, to the readers of *The First Mess*! I still can't believe that I get to make a recipe, post up some photographs, and say hello to you all week after week. The sense of community that you've built up around my little site fills me up with gratitude and constant inspiration. To anyone that has made a recipe or sent me a kind note, this book is for you.

Index

Laura Wright is the writer and photographer behind the highly-acclaimed healthy food blog, *The First Mess*, winner of a 2014 *Saveur* "Best Food Blog" award. In 2016, *The First Mess* was nominated for Best Food Blog in the *Better Homes and Gardens* Blogger Awards. Laura has been featured on several blogs including *The Huffington Post, Saveur, Martha Stewart, Epicurious, Food & Wine, The Washington Post, America's Test Kitchen, The Guardian, The Kitchn, Food52*, and more. She has developed recipes for *Clean Eating Magazine, Food52, Anthropologie.com, BuzzFeed*, and *Pure Green Magazine*. Laura lives in the Niagara region of Southern Ontario, Canada.